# HEMINGWAY

## FOR BEGINNERS

## WRITERS AND READERS PUBLISHING, INC.

P.O. Box 461, Village Station
New York, NY 10014

Writers and Readers Limited
9 Cynthia Street
London N1 9JF
England

•

Text Copyright: © 1994 Errol Selkirk
Illustrations © Anne Finkelstein and James Acevedo
Cover Design: Chris Hyde

A Writers and Readers Documentary Comic Book
Copyright © 1994

ISBN 0-86316-128-6
1 2 3 4 5 6 7 8 9 0

Manufactured in the United States of America

# HEMINGWAY

## FOR BEGINNERS

BY ERROL SELKIRK
ILLUSTRATED BY ANNE FINKELSTEIN
AND JAMES ACEVEDO

# CONTENTS

"The world breaks everyone
and afterwards many are strong at the broken places.
But those that will not break it kills.
It kills the very good and the very gentle
and the very brave impartially.
If you are none of these you can be sure
it will kill you, too,
but there will be no special hurry."

# Ernest Hemingway
# 1899-1961

Decades after his death, Hemingway is still the best-known American writer who ever lived. His style has influenced writers around the world. And the best of his writing continues to set a standard for clarity, power, and vision.

His best-known creation was his own life—what he let the public know of his life. To the public, he was an enviable being who made the entire planet his home, a hero who lived and was prepared to die by his own personal code of honor.

Behind the public mask was an artist, a self more sensitive than he wanted anyone to see. It was the part of him that saw life as it is and suffered for it. And it is this part of him that remains most alive today.

Through his work, Hemingway reveals to us a world stripped of illusion, a world in which men and women struggle to find meaning and some sense of grace. The stakes are high. And the winner takes nothing. But there is no other game in town.

# THE AGE DEMANDED

E rnest Miller Hemingway was born at the dawn of the American Century. The United States had just defeated Spain in a "splendid little war," and America's growing military and industrial might now thrust the nation onto the world stage.

The greatest hero of the Spanish-American War (1898) was Theodore Roosevelt. It was Roosevelt who bravely led his "Rough Riders" to victory up San Juan Hill in Cuba. Two years later, he was elected Vice President of the United States. Then in September 1900, with the assassination of William McKinley, Roosevelt was sworn in as the youngest president in U.S. history.

To young Hemingway, Teddy defined everything that a man of action could be. He was a man of intelligence, soldier, statesman, horseman, big game hunter, world traveler, explorer, naturalist, outdoors man, athlete, and, strangest of all, a popular writer.

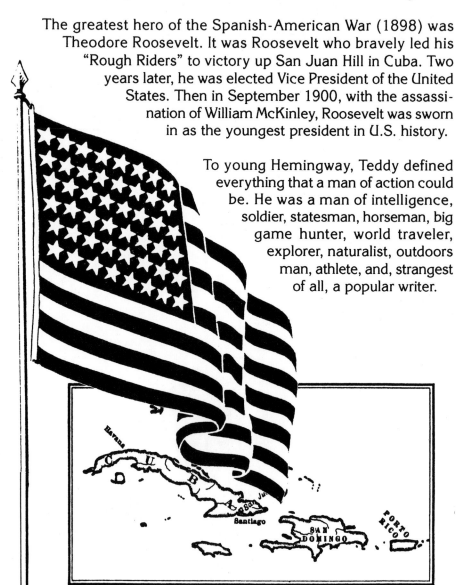

These accomplishments were all the more spectacular since Roosevelt had started life as a sickly child with terrible eyesight. He overcame his weaknesses only through strenuous sports and positive thinking. What boy, reading such a story, would not dream of similar glory for himself?

Hemingway was born on July 21, 1899, the second of six children. His home was Oak Park, Illinois, a suburb of Chicago. His mother, the former Grace Hall, was a tall strong-willed woman. It was she who insisted that the boy be named after her father, whom she called "the finest, purest, noblest man I have ever known."

Ernest always hated his first name. He associated it with the character in foppish Oscar Wilde's play, *The Importance of Being Earnest*. Throughout his life, Hemingway created for himself a stream of nicknames to match his successive identities: The Old Brute, Wemedge, Oinbones, Ernie, Hemingstein, Stein, Hem, E.H., and ultimately, Papa.

About his own Papa, young Ernest had powerful, mixed feelings. Dr. Clarence Edmonds Hemingway was an overworked general practitioner. He was also a strict disciplinarian who had been brought up in a puritanical home, and he scorned vice. He was not a bad looking fellow, but his weak chin seemed to betray some inner lack of character or strength.

In the great outdoors, however, Clarence was transformed, and he took pleasure in teaching Ernest how to fish and hunt. At times he talked about leaving the city forever and taking the family out to the still untamed west. Mother Grace, however, held his romantic aspirations in check.

Grace ruled the roost. As a girl she had been something of a tomboy and had scandalized the town by being the first girl to ride that newfangled invention, the bicycle. Trained as a classical singer, she traveled to New York to study opera. On stage, however, she suffered from severe headaches brought on by stage lights or nervousness. Consequently, she abruptly ended her career, returning to Illinois to marry Dr. Hemingway.

Ernest's birth was preceded eighteen months earlier by that of his sister, Marcelline. For some odd reason, Grace had decided that she wanted to be the mother of twins. So she began to mold both children to fit her desires.

Ernest and his sister slept in the same room in twin white cribs. They had identical dolls and china sets, and later, both learned to sew. Grace even kept Marcelline out of school for a year, so that the two children could be in the same grade.

Baby Hemingway wore frills, bonnets, lace dresses, and stockings. At two years old, Grace was calling her son "Summer Girl." At age three, he and his sister were still wearing identical dresses.

Hemingway called Grace "Fweety" for Sweety. In those days, he was happy to learn his prayers at her knee. His acquiescence, however, became tinged with rebellion. And when Grace once called him her Dutch dolly because of his long hair, Ernest immediately took aim with his finger and shouted:

I NOT A DUTCH DOLLY. I PAWNEE BILL. BANG! I SHOOT FWEETY.

As Ernest grew older, he loved to go to the Field Museum of Natural History in Chicago. There the boy could imagine that he was Teddy Roosevelt on safari, hunting lion, water buffalo, and rhinos.

Each summer the boy got a chance to rough it in the country at the family cottage on Walloon Lake in upper Michigan. The area was still mostly unlogged forests, filled with fish and game and inhabited by impoverished Ojibway Indians.

15

Ernest was taken on his first fishing trip when he was three. He already knew how to handle, load, and shoot a rifle. Dr. Hemingway knew his wood-lore and showed his son where to find various animals and edible plants. Walking through the forest with his father could be an adventure and a delight. But the man had a more frightening side as Hemingway's sister, Marcelline, recalled: "My father's dimpled cheeks and charming smile could change in an instant to the stern, taut mouth and piercing look which was his disciplinary self."

BUT I DIDN'T DO IT!

Dr. Hemingway suffered from black moods throughout his life. When the children misbehaved, they would be thrown across his knee and spanked hard or even beaten with a razor strap, after which they were made to kneel and ask God for forgiveness.

Ernest was still quite young when he began to suffer from the insomnia that would plague him all his life. Frightful thoughts passed through his active imagination as he lay there alone in the dark. Here is a passage Hemingway wrote about ten-year-old Nick Adams, his fictional alter-ego:

"He was not afraid of anything definite as yet. But he was getting very afraid. Then suddenly he was afraid of dying. Just a few weeks before at home, in church, they had sung a hymn, 'Someday the silver cord will break.' While they were singing the hymn, Nick realized that some day he must die. It made him feel quite sick...".

In the darkness, familiar things—even the walls—disappeared. And you disappeared too in a way. Maybe darkness was like death. How could you cling to something as fragile as a thin silver cord? How could you not be afraid? But then what were you? Were you Pawnee Bill or some Dutch dolly? And if you stayed scared, what kind of man would you grow up to be?

Death was one of the long shadows haunting Hemingway. As an adult, Ernest told his own son that the trick to mastering fear was controlling the imagination. He admitted that it was a hard lesson for a boy to master.

For a while Hemingway was able to quiet his own fear of death with the religion of his parents. God's divine message was as clear as day. There was no need for dark mysteries, pagan symbols, bloody sacrifice, or tormented martyrs. The reality of human suffering was balanced by the promise of eternal reward in the life to come. Death was a beginning, not an end. But what comfort was all this to a small boy alone in a dark room?

His friends all admired him. And when he was around, things were never dull. Ernest was a born storyteller, and while on treks in the woods he would amuse them by making up fantastic tales to shout at the trees.

His first published pieces were written for his high school newspaper. Ernest's news stories mostly dramatized the exploits of his friends and himself. He also wrote a column in the first person, "aw shucks" style of humorist Ring Lardner.

Hemingway portrayed his youth as a continual adventure—hiking, hunting, fishing, riding the rails, and sleeping with the occasional Indian maiden. The truth was that he lived a comfortable suburban life. Yet whenever he could, Ernest would take his rifle out past the last houses in town, out to where the prairie began. And though he was practically blind in one eye, he quickly learned how to shoot birds on the wing.

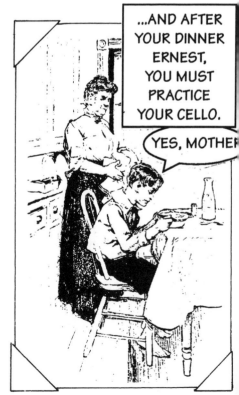

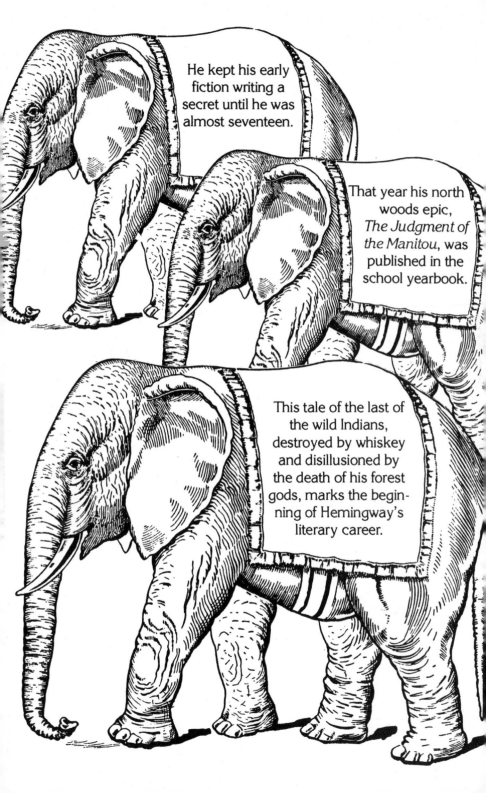

He kept his early fiction writing a secret until he was almost seventeen.

That year his north woods epic, *The Judgment of the Manitou*, was published in the school yearbook.

This tale of the last of the wild Indians, destroyed by whiskey and disillusioned by the death of his forest gods, marks the beginning of Hemingway's literary career.

Hemingway's feelings toward his parents now began to change. More and more he resented his father's harsh discipline. Often he dreamed of turning his shotgun on the man.

Things got worse when the Doctor suffered a nervous collapse and had to take a rest cure. Deeply embarrassed, the boy blamed his domineering mother for making Clarence such a weakling.

To compensate, the boy enrolled in a boxing class. On the first day, he almost got his nose broken, but he kept at it.

In time Ernest developed a powerful punch and a few good moves. Though his bad eyes and slow reflexes were a liability, he became a capable brawler who wasn't afraid to use dirty tricks to win. Throughout adolescence and for the rest of his life, he relied on his skill as a fighter to settle accounts, real and imaginary.

Yet bigger battles were being fought overseas. America entered World War I in 1917. It was only natural that Ernest wanted to join the fight to make the world safe for democracy. But Dr. Hemingway had other ideas.

Clarence offered to use family connections to get his son a reporter's job on a prestigious newspaper, *The Kansas City Star*. Ernest agreed. This would begin his apprenticeship in writing. With those first lessons learned, Hemingway would at last come face to face with death.

# IN ANOTHER COUNTRY

GOING MY WAY BIG BOY?

Kansas City, Missouri, was a rough, raucous town back in the autumn of 1917. Twenty–odd blocks of K.C. were lined with wild, smoky dives like the Bucket of Blood, where brass knuckles were as popular as pickled pigs knuckles and beer. Further downtown was a row of lively burlesque houses. Street-walkers and soldier boys from nearby Fort Leavenworth mingled to the sound of rattling silver dollars and ragtime jazz.

Hemingway was kept busy. When he wasn't at the *Star*, he was out riding in police cars and ambulances. He covered fires, accidents, epidemics, and crimes. He got to know his way around city hall, the hospital, the morgue, and the loud bars. Friends soon noticed his incredible vitality. Ernest could work all day, finish off a jug of wine, and talk into the night. Next morning at dawn, he'd wake up ready to take on the world.

The young reporter was fascinated by this raw, violent city:

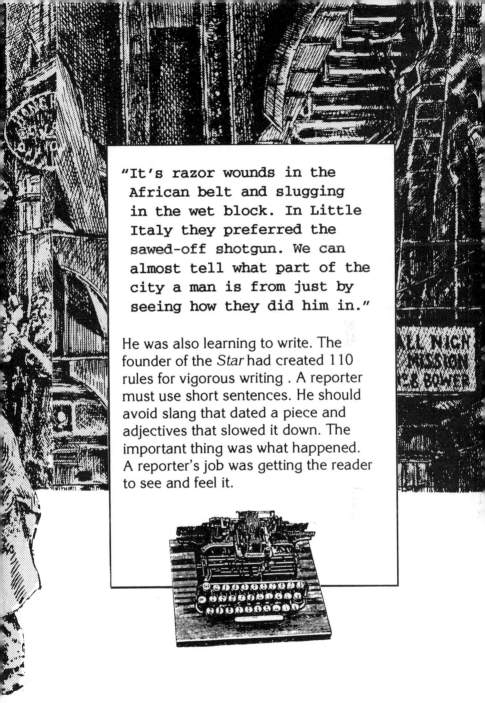

"It's razor wounds in the African belt and slugging in the wet block. In Little Italy they preferred the sawed-off shotgun. We can almost tell what part of the city a man is from just by seeing how they did him in."

He was also learning to write. The founder of the *Star* had created 110 rules for vigorous writing . A reporter must use short sentences. He should avoid slang that dated a piece and adjectives that slowed it down. The important thing was what happened. A reporter's job was getting the reader to see and feel it.

It was at the *Star* that Ernest met Ted Brumback, a reporter who'd already driven along the French Front. Brumback told stories that stirred the young man's desire to get overseas before all the shooting stopped.

Hemingway signed up with the Red Cross ambulance service in 1918. He was given the honorary rank of Second Lieutenant and assigned to an ambulance unit on the Italian Front. The Red Cross issued him an officer's uniform, which Ernest immediately supplemented with a dashing pair of high cordovan boots.

Hemingway who always had an active imagination, wrote his family that he'd met the famous actress Mae Marsh—and was now engaged to her. His parents agonized over this news. Grace Hemingway worried about her son's recklessness and wrote to him in the sappy language of the time, of her ideal of marriage:

*bo,*
*comp*
*a lit*
*a bit*
*soofed*
*walled u*
*just two*
*souls.*

*Love*
*Moth*

Ernest fired off a telegram which explained everything in no uncertain terms:

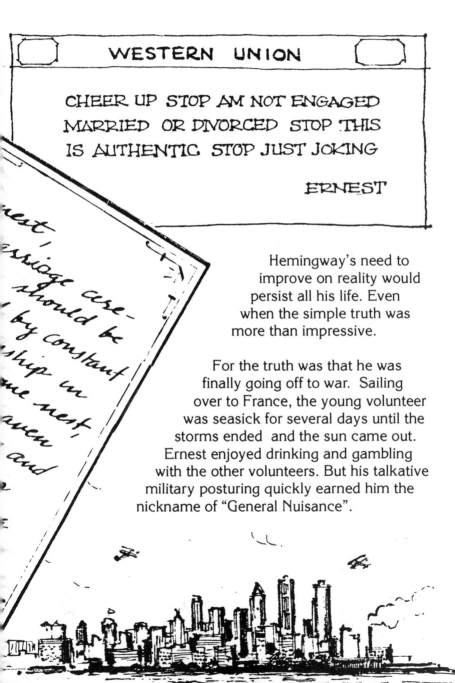

WESTERN UNION

CHEER UP STOP AM NOT ENGAGED MARRIED OR DIVORCED STOP THIS IS AUTHENTIC STOP JUST JOKING

ERNEST

Hemingway's need to improve on reality would persist all his life. Even when the simple truth was more than impressive.

For the truth was that he was finally going off to war. Sailing over to France, the young volunteer was seasick for several days until the storms ended and the sun came out. Ernest enjoyed drinking and gambling with the other volunteers. But his talkative military posturing quickly earned him the nickname of "General Nuisance".

As soon as he hit Paris, Hemingway hired a cab to take him out to the action. The Germans were shelling the city from seventy miles away. The nervous driver followed the sound of the explosions until a shell screeched overhead and took a chunk out of the famous church on Place de la Madelaine. Hemingway, satisfied that he had arrived in a war zone, headed for a hotel.

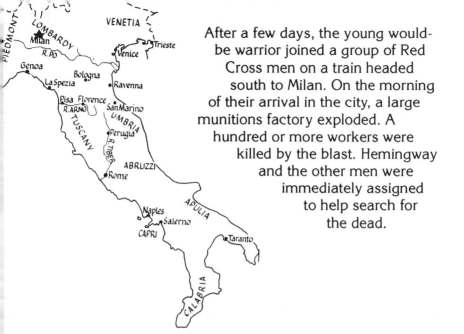

After a few days, the young would-be warrior joined a group of Red Cross men on a train headed south to Milan. On the morning of their arrival in the city, a large munitions factory exploded. A hundred or more workers were killed by the blast. Hemingway and the other men were immediately assigned to help search for the dead.

This was not the glorious warfare he had imagined back home. The volunteers began by collecting whole bodies. Then they were told to collect fragments, some of which had been impaled on the barbed wire around the factory. It was an introduction to war Hemingway would not soon forget.

Hemingway was sent to an ambulance unit based in Schio, a small town east of Milan. The young lieutenant's duties involved driving the top heavy Fiat trucks filled with wounded down a mountain to the closest aid station. The fighting in this sector was light. Most of the casualties suffered from dysentery or self-inflicted wounds.

Ernest was billeted in an old factory building, which the men jokingly called the Country Club. In the evening, officers were served plenty of strong red wine, stewed game, and pasta.

"There's nothing here but scenery, and too damn much of that. I'm going to get out of this ambulance section and see if I can find where the war is."

Hemingway volunteered to serve on the Piave River Front, just north of Venice. The fighting was much heavier there. But Hemingway's job was less than heroic. He was simply expected to bicycle up to the Front with cigarettes and chocolate for the fighting men.

On the eighth of July 1918, the young man finally found his war. It was close to midnight. Hemingway was in the forward trenches passing out goodies when a large Austrian mortar shell filled with shrapnel detonated just a few feet away.

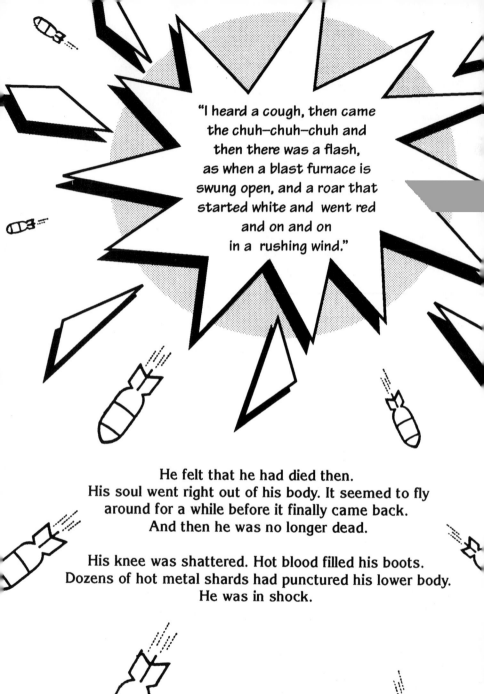

"I heard a cough, then came
the chuh–chuh–chuh and
then there was a flash,
as when a blast furnace is
swung open, and a roar that
started white and went red
and on and on
in a rushing wind."

He felt that he had died then.
His soul went right out of his body. It seemed to fly
around for a while before it finally came back.
And then he was no longer dead.

His knee was shattered. Hot blood filled his boots.
Dozens of hot metal shards had punctured his lower body.
He was in shock.

Some people today believe that after the explosion Hemingway somehow threw a wounded soldier over his shoulder and carried him back to an aid station. According to this version, Austrian machine guns caught him in the open, hit him twice—in the shoulder and the leg—and knocked him down. Still he managed to continue on to safety.

This story Hemingway wrote to his parents and told others. Ten years later, Hemingway had second thoughts, objecting when his publisher's publicity department portrayed him as a hero. He feared it would make him seem like a fool or a liar to those who knew the facts. A different version of the story appears in Hemingway's World War I novel, *A Farewell to Arms*. The young Red Cross lieutenant in the book is blown up while eating cheese. And as for heroism:

**"I didn't carry anyone. I couldn't move."**

Hero or not, the nineteen-year-old officer was quickly rushed from the front and taken to a hospital in Milan. It was here that he met the first real love of his life.

Nurse Agnes von Kurowsky was an "older" woman of twenty–six. She was from Baltimore. Tall and shapely, with long chestnut colored hair, Agnes had an aggressive, provocative charm. Ernest fell for her immediately. And she soon found herself drawn to this handsome young patient.

At first, Agnes dismissed Ernest's love as youthful infatuation. To put him in his place, she insisted on calling him "Kid." When he was well enough to walk about on crutches, Agnes went with him to explore the shops in town, the race track, the cafes, and restaurants. She ignored the brandy bottles Hemingway smuggled in to deaden the pain of his wounds. After all, they were in love. Weren't they?

And they were going to get married. This is what he excitedly wrote friends back home. All he had to do was return to America, find a job, and save up some cash. Unfortunately, Agnes was transferred across Italy to a hospital in Florence. And everything changed.

Hemingway's legs finally healed. But he still suffered other, less obvious wounds. He was still badly shell shocked. He recalled the feeling in a story called "Now I Lay Me":

"I myself did not want to sleep because I had been living for a long time with the knowledge that if I ever shut my eyes in the dark and let myself go, my soul would go out of my body."

A final Italian offensive was massing to the north. Hemingway, still very shaky, volunteered to go back to the Front, but a case of jaundice sent him back to the hospital.

The war ended on November 11, 1918. He had only managed to see Agnes a couple times since she had been transferred.

On the night of the Armistice, a lonely Lieutenant Hemingway was back in Milan, drinking with Edward "Chink" Dorman Smith, a heavily decorated British officer.

Ernest, bragging about his fictional exploits as an infantry officer commanding Italian troops, lied shamelessly to the seasoned veteran. Chink, in a calm, understated way, modestly mentioned a few of his own experiences in France. Some of these later wound up in Hemingway's fiction, and he would adopt a similar cool, ironic tone in some of his writing. Yet he must have felt somewhat uncomfortable there, trading stories with a real hero. Years later he wrote:

**"I had been wounded, it was true;
but we all knew that being wounded, after all,
was really an accident."**

There was nothing heroic about getting hit while passing out cigarettes and chocolate as a gentleman volunteer. He knew there was a difference between himself and the real war heroes. They all seemed detached, resolute, and powerful as hunting hawks:

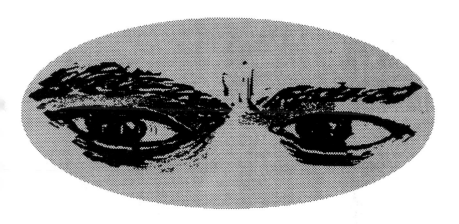

"And I was not a hawk; although I might seem like a hawk to those who had never hunted."

Now he would return to America. And there he would make himself seem like a hawk among sparrows.

# SOLDIER'S HOME

The handsome young man, supporting himself with a cane, limped slowly down the gang plank. He was wearing his sleek, tailored uniform with a short black cape and high, shiny military boots. He looked like a hero.

A news reporter jumped at the chance to interview him. An article in the January 22, 1919, *New York Sun,* stated that Hemingway had: "...probably more scars than any other man in or out of uniform who defied the shrapnel of the Central Powers."

The article went on to say that he was hit by 227 pieces of enemy steel and that he bravely returned to the Front when his wounds healed. This was America's first published encounter with the Hemingway legend.

Ernest came home to Oak Park. He showed off his uniform and medals and waited anxiously for each of Agnes' letters. By March she told him not to write so much or so often.

Within a month she admitted to having an affair with an older man, an Italian officer—a Duke of all things—who had asked her to marry him.

The young veteran was shattered. She was his first love. Nothing had changed in America. But he had changed. None of the girls his age could understand him. Hemingway started drinking and sometimes kept on drinking until he passed out. And he began to write about his experiences in the war.

Dressed in his uniform, h[...]
told his stories to an aud[...]
ence at his old high schoo[...]
He regaled the crowd wi[...]
tales of infantry officers s[...]
tough that they plugged u[...]
bullet holes in their bodi[...]
with cigarettes and ke[...]
right on fighting. Final[...]
Ernest spoke of his ow[...]
wounds and held up [...]
medal he claimed that t[...]
King of Italy had awarde[...]
him personally.

These were exaggerations, if not outright lies. But the folks back home had already heard too many wild stories about the war. To be listened to at all, Hemingway felt he had to lie. Most of lies consisted of attributing to himself what others had done. But the lying soon began to disgust him.

Hemingway clearly suffered from the delayed effects of combat stress. He could only sleep with a night light on in the room and then only if he had plenty of alcohol in his system. Much later, he confessed to how he felt during and after the war:

"I was hurt bad all the way through and I was really spooked at the end."

He was also growing further and further from his family. Their values, their cozy religion, even the high-flown language they used to express their feelings offended him. Ernest remembered only too well the terms used during the war to harangue the troops before the senseless slaughter of battle: Glory, Honor, Sacrifice.

The war changed all that for him. The false pomp and sentimentality of the Victorian Age had died in that trench, when an explosion rendered body and soul. The harsh reality of the modern world was still to be discovered—or invented.

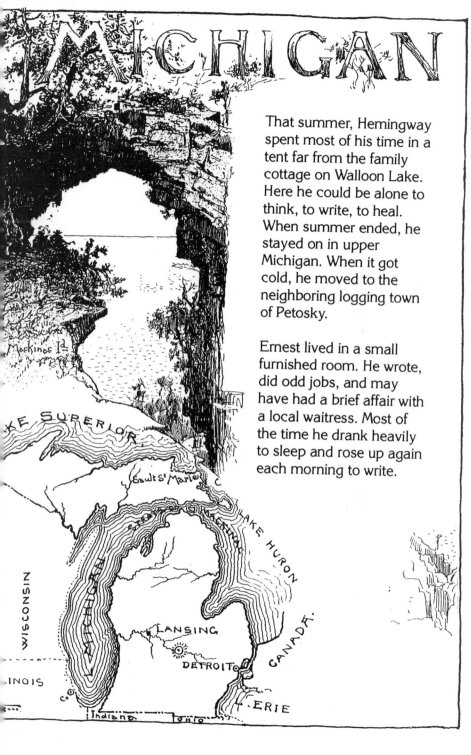

# MICHIGAN

That summer, Hemingway spent most of his time in a tent far from the family cottage on Walloon Lake. Here he could be alone to think, to write, to heal. When summer ended, he stayed on in upper Michigan. When it got cold, he moved to the neighboring logging town of Petosky.

Ernest lived in a small furnished room. He wrote, did odd jobs, and may have had a brief affair with a local waitress. Most of the time he drank heavily to sleep and rose up again each morning to write.

Years later he cap-
tured the desperation
he was feeling in a
remarkable story,
"The Killers." It's
about a man with no
place left to run, who
lies in bed with his
face to the wall, wait-
ing for death to over-
take him.

One evening in Petosky, Ernest gave one of his war lectures to a local women's group and met Mrs. Harriet Connable, a rich and influential Canadian lady who made him an unusual offer. She was looking for a tutor for her disabled son. If Hemingway agreed to help, he could have room, board, and a small salary.

To sweeten the deal, Mrs. Connable promised that her husband would try to get the young veteran a writing job on the prestigious *Toronto Star Weekly*.

An editor on the paper described Hemingway as a large, loose limbed youth who limped a bit and leaned on a walking stick. The young man was simultaneously shy and restless. He perspired a great deal and seemed fixated on his war experiences. The editor concluded:

" A more weird combination of quivering
sensitiveness and preoccupation with violence
surely never walked the earth."

The new *Toronto Star* reporter could write though. Ernest reported on varied topics—from how to grow a military mustache that could make you look like a war hero even if you were a shirker to how to find the best rainbow trout fishing in the world without getting eaten alive by mosquitoes.

His tone was often humorous, even wry. Always he succeeded in conveying the impression that he was a complete authority, writing from long experience on the subject—whatever it was. This gift he would have all his life.

It was now the second summer
after the war. Hemingway left
Canada and again traveled to
Walloon Lake. This would be a
lifelong pattern. One home in the
winter, another in the summer.

Shortly after his twenty-first birthday, Hemingway's younger sisters, Ursula and Sunny, held a party that Hemingway and a friend attended. When everyone returned late to the cottage, Grace Hemingway accused her son of corrupting the girls.

Ernest reacted angrily, and Grace handed him a letter which she had written earlier. In it she compared a mother's love to a bank account. Ernest was overdrawn. She accused him of being a lazy drunk and pleasure seeker, neglecting his duties to God and Savior. Ernest moved to a nearby boarding house.

Years later he would write about a similar confrontation between mother and son. The young man in the story "Soldier's Home" had also just returned from the war and finds it hard to adjust. His mother insists that everyone must find his rightful place in God's Kingdom. The youth replies:

## "I'm not in His Kingdom."

That fall, Hemingway moved to Chicago. He continued writing freelance articles for the *Toronto Star*. But most of them now focused on the growing gang violence that resulted from Prohibition.

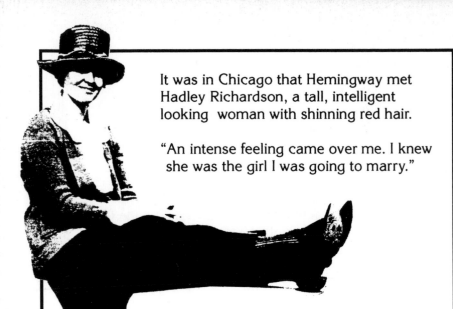

It was in Chicago that Hemingway met Hadley Richardson, a tall, intelligent looking woman with shinning red hair.

"An intense feeling came over me. I knew she was the girl I was going to marry."

Hadley's life had been filled with catastrophe. She'd spent a year in a wheelchair as a child; her father had shot himself; she had a mental breakdown on a family trip to Europe and later had to withdraw from Bryn Mawr College because of depression. More recently, her sister had died in a freak fire. Then her mother, who insisted on keeping Hadley by her side, wasted away from Bright's Disease.

Hadley visited Chicago shortly after the funeral. Ernest met her at a party, and for the next three weeks, they saw each other constantly.

Hemingway couldn't stop thinking about returning to Europe. Now he began talking about taking Hadley with him to Italy. She was flattered by the attentions of this handsome young fellow. But he had zero money, and she wanted a man that she could look up to and respect.

Hemingway decided to dig in. He took a job as editor for *Cooperative Commonwealth* magazine. Actually, it was part of a racket that defrauded investors out of millions. The young man looked the other way for as long as he could, saving money, and converting it to Italian lira.

By early 1921, Ernest was complaining of black moods and suicidal feelings. The work at the magazine was getting to him. And he missed Hadley terribly. His gloom can still be felt in the poems he wrote at the time:

> It is cool on the roofs of the city
> The city sweats
> Dripping and stark.
> Maggots of life
> Crawl in the hot loneliness of the city
> Love curdles in the city
> Love songs in the hot whispering from the pavements...

Hemingway was still confused about himself, about the war, and about his family. But he was clear about one thing: he wanted to leave America. He was fed up with its puritanical attitudes towards drinking and sex, its crushing conformity, and its veneration of business and money. The land and its people simply had no romance.

"Don't mind fighting and dying for this great country. Just don't want to live here."

One evening in Chicago, Hemingway met a man who would help change his life—a writer by the name of Sherwood Anderson.

Now in his forties, Anderson had literally walked away from a successful career as factory president to become a writer. His most famous work, *Winesburg, Ohio*, was a unique collection of linked short stories depicting life in a small Midwestern town. The main character in the book was a sensitive young man who longed to escape into the wide world.

Hemingway immediately responded to the theme of the book. He also admired Anderson's clear, simple language, and the understated yet powerful way the writer conveyed emotion through the use of details. Anderson in turn liked Hemingway and his writing:

"A young fellow of extraordinary talent...instinctively in touch with everything worthwhile going on."

On the third of September 1921, Hemingway and Hadley—whom he'd already nicknamed "Hash"—were married up at Walloon Lake. Younger brother Leicester Hemingway, now seven, swore that Ernie's knees were visibly knocking as he walked down the aisle.

When the couple returned to Chicago, they began to add up their resources and plan for their trip abroad.

Hadley received a comfortable $3000 a year from a trust fund.
And Hemingway had also been able to save some money while
working as an editor.

He still hoped to write freelance articles for the *Toronto Star*,
datelined Paris, but to his surprise, the newspaper actually hired
him as their first European correspondent. Everything had
almost miraculously fallen into place.

Anderson graciously gave Hemingway letters of introduction to
James Joyce, Gertrude Stein, and to a gifted, eccentric
expatriate poet, Ezra Pound. Ernest didn't realize it yet, but all
three would help him find his place in the literature of the world.

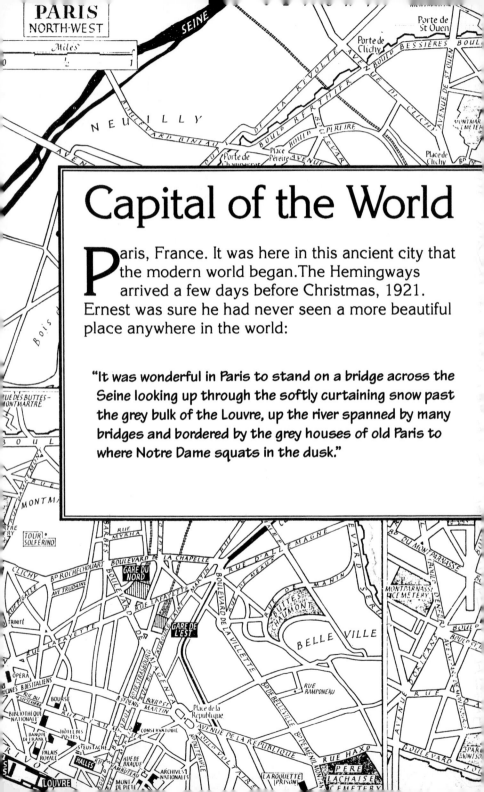

# Capital of the World

**P**aris, France. It was here in this ancient city that the modern world began. The Hemingways arrived a few days before Christmas, 1921. Ernest was sure he had never seen a more beautiful place anywhere in the world:

"It was wonderful in Paris to stand on a bridge across the Seine looking up through the softly curtaining snow past the grey bulk of the Louvre, up the river spanned by many bridges and bordered by the grey houses of old Paris to where Notre Dame squats in the dusk."

Yet it was a beauty tinged with tragedy. The Great War had ended only three years before. Half of Europe was still in rubble. Twenty million lay buried under stone markers that seemed to stretch from one end of the continent to the other.

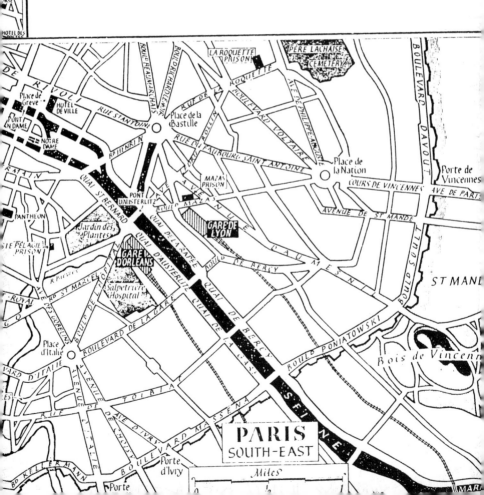

PARIS
SOUTH-EAST

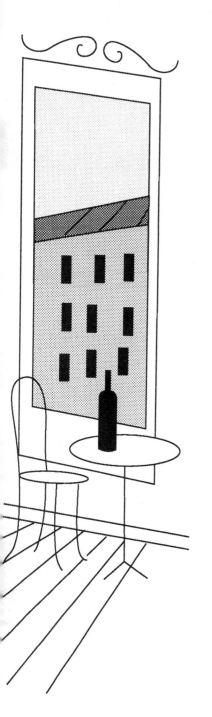

He found a cheap two-room flat in a dank old building in a rough, working class quarter of the city. Every floor had a rude squat toilet in the hall. For Hadley, who was used to a more refined style of life in Saint Louis, the place held little charm.

The young writer made his studio in a room on the narrow rue Mouffetard, in a rundown hotel, where he claimed that symbolist poet Paul Verlaine died. It was there that he began to write his first mature stories.

The couple soon got settled into Paris. Hadley practiced Ravel and Brahms on the piano they rented. Hemingway began to teach himself French. He practiced what he learned at a race track at Auteuil, where he traded sporting stories, tips, and colorful expressions with the jockeys and touts. A few years later, he would use the atmosphere he absorbed for one of his best early stories, *My Old Man*.

But he was also a working newsman. One of his first articles was an attack against the hordes of American bohemians already descending upon the city. They were attracted by the artistic ambiance of the Latin Quarter and by how cheap everything was in post-War France.

Hemingway bitterly mocked this "strange-looking breed" who spent hours in smoky cafes pretending to be avant-garde artists. Their careless individuality of dress seemed to him a uniform of eccentricity. They wasted in talk, the energy and time real artists need for work. Worst of all, they produced nothing.

In contrast, Hemingway was now totally committed to writing. One of the first to encourage him was fellow American Sylvia Beach. She had recently founded Shakespeare & Company, a unique English-language bookstore and lending library. Here Ernest discovered books by Whitman, Poe, Conrad, and D.H. Lawrence, as well as translations of great Russian writers like Turgenev, Tolstoy, and Dostoyevsky. Reading these authors and others helped complete the education that he had missed by not going to college.

Ms. Beach was also the first to publish James Joyce's visionary novel, *Ulysses*. Through her, Hemingway was introduced to the brilliant, near-sighted Irishman. Ernest was impressed. Joyce was a true modern. His writing was lyrical, rich and multi-layered as the universe itself. He was one of the first to capture the inner lives of his characters through the use of what is today called "stream of consciousness." And he was frank about sexual matters.

Joyce quickly befriended Hemingway. Sometimes when they went out drinking, Joyce enjoyed using his wit to provoke fights with strangers. It was always handy to have the tough young American around to tell:

"Deal with him, Hemingway. Deal with him."

Ernest found an unlikely sparring partner in the person of another true modern, American poet Ezra Pound.

Pound didn't look modern, though. He looked more like a character in an old-fashioned opera. Hemingway mocked the man's eccentric appearance: his little untrimmed goatee, his flamboyant open-necked shirts, and his broad brimmed slouch hat. But soon he realized that Ezra was an original, the real thing. His religion was literature. And his mission was to restore to the English language the beauty and power of the spoken word.

Pound helped Ernest make his writing sharper, more concise. Once he had been an advisor to the poet T.S. Elliot. Now he was teaching Hemingway to create concrete images that produced emotion. In return for Pound's coaching, Hemingway taught the poet the manly art of self-defense.

Not everyone in Paris, though, shared the young American's favorable view of Pound:

"He is like a village explainer.
Excellent if you were a village,
but if you were not, not."

—Gertrude Stein

Mention Joyce's name twice at Gertrude Stein's home,
Hemingway remarked, and you were not welcome back.
Mention Pound's name once, and the result would likely be the
same.

Ms. Stein was a Jewish American from San Francisco. She
naturally resented Ezra Pound's outspoken anti-semitism. Like
many intellectuals of the time, he believed that Jews were
responsible for everything from the rise in interest rates to the
biblical Fall of Man.

But it was the religion of literature that really made them enemies. Ms. Stein insisted on being the absolute center of the literary universe that radiated outward from her comfortable home at 27 rue de Fleurus.

Hemingway liked sitting next to Ms. Stein, listening to her grand pronouncements about art and life while sampling the tasty little cakes and the lively colored liqueurs provided by the *maison*. On the walls were enough fine paintings for a small museum. Here were some of the best works of Matisse, Cézanne, Toulouse-Lautrec, and naturally, her good friend, Picasso, who had painted her famous portrait.

"Something had been coming out of him, certainly it had been coming out of him, certainly it was something certainly it had been coming out of him and it had meaning..."

"Modern literature is

Stein had inherited money. She was able to live comfortably with her lifelong companion, Alice Toklas, insulated from the demands of the public. Her objective was revolutionary.

Her Cubist painter friends had freed art from traditional meaning. Now Stein would do the same for literature. Language would be approached like a kind of music, dependent on rhythm and repetition of theme.

Repetition was one of the techniques Hemingway learned from her. But Ms. Stein was a demanding teacher:

"It used to be easy before I met you. I certainly was bad, gosh, I'm awfully bad now but it's a different kind of bad."

rtrude Stein." —Gertrude Stein

She suggested that Hemingway get out of newspaper work as soon as possible. Otherwise, she warned, he would never actually see things, only words. Yet it was as a newsman that Hemingway traveled most of the 10,000 miles he covered his first couple years in Europe.

Hemingway met many of the leaders of the post-War world at international peace conferences held in Genoa and Lausanne. He also learned a new form of communication, cablese, the shorthand that correspondents use to send news stories over the telegraph.

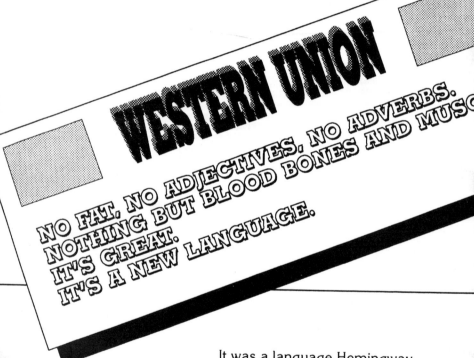

WESTERN UNION

NO FAT, NO ADJECTIVES, NO ADVERBS. NOTHING BUT BLOOD BONES AND MUSC IT'S GREAT. IT'S A NEW LANGUAGE.

It was a language Hemingway would quickly master and put to use in his fiction. He was also talking to senior correspondents from the socialist press, men such as Lincoln Steffens and Max Eastman. They helped the young reporter to see through the smokescreen of diplomatic propaganda, to the economic and political forces that actually shape events.

Yet Hemingway was never much interested in political abstractions. He soon turned his sharp eye to the politicians themselves. And he was one of the first to condemn Benito Mussolini, the Italian Fascist leader.

The young reporter interviewed "Il Duce" in 1922. Musolini was sitting at a desk with a wolf cub at his side, staring intently at a book, which he happened to be holding upside down. Hemingway published a news story which astutely called the Fascist leader "the biggest bluff in Europe." Hemingway concluded, "There is something wrong, even histrionically, with a man who wears white spats with a black shirt."

YES MASTER!

The *Toronto Star* ordered Hemingway to travel to Turkey, where a hopeless war with Greece was coming to its inevitable, bloody conclusion. Hadley begged him not to go. But he went anyway.

The Greek army had fought bravely against the Turks. But they were now commanded by incompetent officers who ordered troops to advance into their own artillery fire. The Greek lines collapsed. There was panic. A massive retreat began as millions of civilians fled their homes. Hemingway saw horrors that eclipsed his memories of the fighting in Italy:

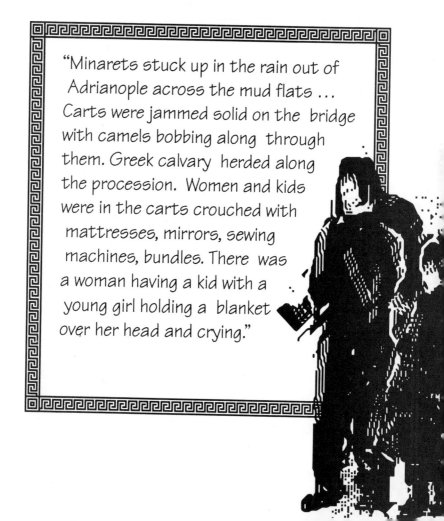

"Minarets stuck up in the rain out of Adrianople across the mud flats ... Carts were jammed solid on the bridge with camels bobbing along through them. Greek calvary herded along the procession. Women and kids were in the carts crouched with mattresses, mirrors, sewing machines, bundles. There was a woman having a kid with a young girl holding a blanket over her head and crying."

He returned to Paris exhausted, sick with malaria and so covered with bug bites and lice that he had to have his head shaved. Hadley quickly forgave him. But within a month, Ernest was off to yet another international conference. And another crisis, even more serious, was about to overtake the couple.

Hadley arranged to meet her husband in Switzerland when his assignment was over. She figured that Ernest might want to work on his stories when he wasn't skiing. So she packed them all in a valise—which was then stolen from her train compartment. When she met Hemingway, she was hysterical.

I'm *so* sorry!

Not only had she packed his stories, she'd also packed his carbon copies. Now Ernest would have to start over as a writer. And he found it hard to forgive.

Hemingway was always tough on people he trusted when he thought they failed him. From the mountains of Switzerland he wrote Pound that the high altitude had robbed him of his sexual desire. Was he falling out of love? The couple apparently worked things out. A few months later, Hadley was pregnant.

Hemingway complained bitterly to Gertrude Stein that he was too young to be a father. Ms. Stein laughed. The rest of that second winter in Europe was grim.

Late in the spring, Ms. Stein encouraged Hemingway to take a trip to Spain. A bullfight might be just the thing he needed. She couldn't have been more right.

Writer Robert McAlmon accompanied him to Madrid. McAlmon was a poet and the publisher of some of Hemingway's earliest work. He drank hard, had a sharp eye, an acid tongue, and an overwhelming skepticism.

McAlmon recalled how Hemingway stared at the "maggot-eaten corpse of a dog" lying on a railway platform in Spain. Ernest told him that he had seen many such horrors during the war. And that it was up to the young men of their generation to take a detached and scientific attitude towards reality and death. McAlmon thought this self-hardening process was just another example of Hemingway's phony bravado.

DAMN

James Joyce was more understanding. Joyce believed that McAlmon pretended to be sensitive. And Hemingway pretended to be tough. But the truth was actually the other way around.

Bull fighting was a revelation to Hemingway. It was not a sport. It was more like a brutal Greek play in which the hero was torn apart by the furies or was forced to blind himself. Bull fighting was a tragedy.

"He drew out the sword from the folds of the muleta and sighted with the same movement and called to the bull, Toro! Toro! and the bull charged and Villalta charged and just for a moment they became one. Villalta became one with the bull and then it was over."

A bullfight was like having a ringside seat at war, but nothing was going to happen to you. Hemingway wrote that it was the only place where you could still see life and death—violent death—now that the war was over. As a writer, this experience was invaluable.

"I was trying to learn to write, commencing with the simplest things, and one of the simplest things of all and the most fundamental is violent death."

Hemingway plunged himself into the craft of the matador. He roomed at a pension frequented by bullfighters and their assistants. Soon he was learning spicy, conversational Spanish and the technical terminology of the *corrida de torros*. Whatever he did, Hemingway was driven to become an expert.

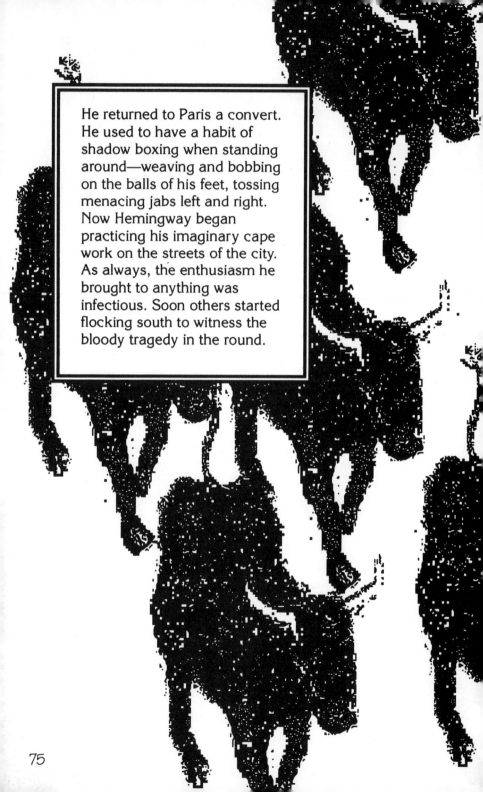

He returned to Paris a convert. He used to have a habit of shadow boxing when standing around—weaving and bobbing on the balls of his feet, tossing menacing jabs left and right. Now Hemingway began practicing his imaginary cape work on the streets of the city. As always, the enthusiasm he brought to anything was infectious. Soon others started flocking south to witness the bloody tragedy in the round.

In July, he took Hadley to Pamplona for the running of the bulls. Hemingway tested his courage by letting the bulls chase him through the streets of this picturesque Spanish mountain town. He even jumped down in the bull ring with a horde of other amateurs. McAlmon saw it all:

> "Hemingway took a charge straight on face, and then, catching the steer's horns, attempted to throw it. He did break its strength and got cheered by the crowd."

The trip to Spain seemed an appropriate way to say goodbye to Europe. Already five months pregnant, Hadley had persuaded Hemingway to have the child in North America, where the medical care was better. Reluctantly the father-to-be arranged for a full-time position working on the *Toronto Star*.

*PAPA!*

John Hadley Nicanor Hemingway was born in October of 1923. His odd middle name came from a bullfighter that the Hemingways admired in Pamplona, Nicanor Villalta. Ernest was on a train rushing north from assignment in New York when the boy, nicknamed "Bumby", came into the world.

Soon as the new father arrived in town, he dashed straight to Hadley in the hospital. His editor at the *Toronto Star* was Mr. Harry Hindmarsh. Hindmarsh wanted no prima donas on his staff. He tried to put Ernest in his place, giving him too many assignments, too often, and too far away from home.

Hemingway was miserable. Toronto was frigid, gray, and provincial compared to Paris. There was no time to write stories. And the baby kept him up at night. The only good news was that his writing was just coming out in several slim volumes published in Europe.

# SOMETHING

Ernest's parents were some of the first to read the new fiction he'd been writing. They were shocked and disgusted. One of the stories, seemingly autobiographical, involved a bitter young war veteran who was jilted by the girl he loved overseas. In desperation, he picks up a streetwalker and contracts a venereal disease in the back of a taxi.

It was soon obvious that returning to North America had been a mistake. Hemingway abruptly quit his job at the *Star*. He and his little family sailed for France in December 1923. No longer could he depend on a correspondent's pay to make ends meet. From now on he would have to make a living as a writer of fiction.

Hemingway found an apartment. The place had no electricity, only rudimentary plumbing and a noisy sawmill next door, but nearby was a comfortable workers' cafe, the Closerie des Lilas. Here he could be left alone to write.

In his new stories, Ernest was experimenting with eliminating details to heighten the effect on the reader. The trick was to make people feel more than they understood:

> "I always try to write on the principle of the iceberg. There is seven-eighths of it underwater for every part that shows. Anything you know you can eliminate and it only strengthens the iceberg. It's the part that doesn't show."

He now began to write about Nick Adams, a young man very similar to himself, in the story called "The Big-Two–Hearted River."

The time is right after the war. The northern Michigan country-side is burned out, a wasteland. The nearby village is a ghost town. Nick has to hike far through the blackened brush to reach good fishing ground. He is disturbed and deeply frightened by something. To maintain his grip, he tries to stop thinking. He focuses his full attention on every act. He moves slowly, deliberately. He carefully puts his camp in order. Each action is precise.

All we know is that Nick is unsettled by the night mist flowing from the swamp on the opposite bank of the river. And that he is terrified by the prospect of fishing there:

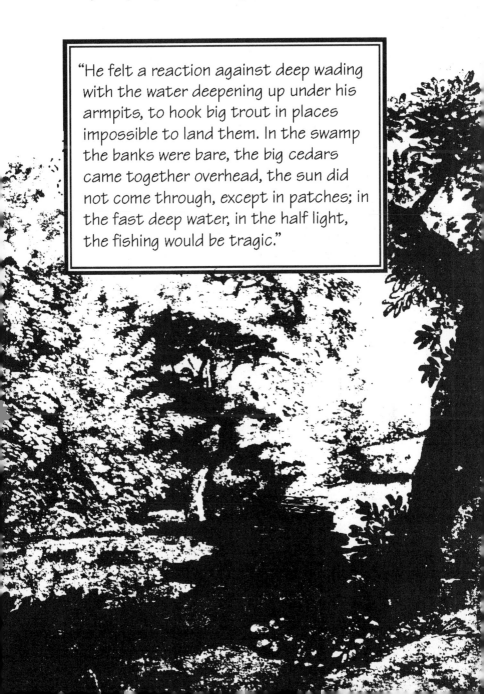

"He felt a reaction against deep wading with the water deepening up under his armpits, to hook big trout in places impossible to land them. In the swamp the banks were bare, the big cedars came together overhead, the sun did not come through, except in patches; in the fast deep water, in the half light, the fishing would be tragic."

The effect of this technique was to make Nick's state of mind disturbingly concrete. The mist and the uncharted swamp seem as ominous as the memories he wants to escape. Yet the cause of his fear is never mentioned. This was a new kind of storytelling that impressed other writers:

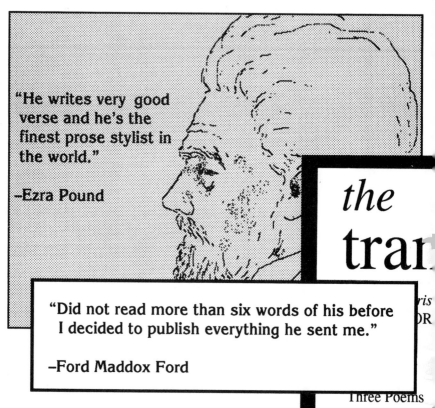

"He writes very good verse and he's the finest prose stylist in the world."

–Ezra Pound

*the*
tran

"Did not read more than six words of his before I decided to publish everything he sent me."

–Ford Maddox Ford

Three Poems

In the Garde
Marc Krantz
July
Herriot In the
The Making of

NEW YORK:
Thomas Selze
50 c.

Ford Maddox Ford was a well-known English novelist then living in Paris. He was also the publisher of *the transatlantic review,* an influential little magazine that printed some of the best of the post-war writers. It was Ford who declared to the world that Hemingway's style was as new and clean as pebbles fresh from a brook.

Ernest disliked the man's fat, pink face, his dirty, rumpled suits, and his habit of mumbling his words—a pretense that Ford must have associated with the English country squire he seemed to style himself on.

Yet Hemingway was quite ready to forget all that if it meant getting published in the *t.a.*, and he was even more happy when Ford asked him to help edit the magazine. One of the first things he did was to type out a large chunk of Gertrude Stein's writing and get it into print. This was an act of respect and gratitude that Ms. Stein never forgot—even years later when their friendship was strained.

Vol. II. No. 2
August 1924

tlantic
review

Bryher

by Richardson
Nathan Asch
Dos Passos
Guy Hickok
Gertrude Stein

PARIS:
Transatlantic Review Co.
7 FRS. 50

Money was definitely short in the Hemingway home. Ernest received no pay from his job at the *t.a.*, and Hadley's trust fund had suffered from bad investments back in America. To raise cash, Ernest sparred with boxers for ten francs a round.

Somehow he always found money for travel. In July of 1924, Hem, Hadley, and a gang of friends descended on Pamplona for the fiesta:

"The godamdest wild time and fun you ever saw. Everybody in town lit for a week, bulls racing loose through the streets every morning, dancing and fireworks all night...and us guys practically the guest of the city."

—Hemingway

Hemingway's enthusiasm was infectious. One of his pals jumped down into the arena with the other bullfight aficionados. A bull tossed the young man into the air and caused him to suffer a couple of fractured ribs. Ernest quickly leaped in to coax the bull away.

In the July 29th edition of the *Chicago Tribune*, Hemingway's hometown paper, this headline appeared:

**BULL GORES 2 YANKS ACTING AS TOREADORS**

The paper mentioned him by name and said that while saving a friend from getting mauled, he had a close brush with death. Whether or not Ernest dictated the story to a reporter sitting in Paris, we will never know.

Hemingway returned to Paris as reviews of his first fiction collection, *In Our Time*, began to appear. The typeface used for the title was supposed to make the work seem more "modern." Modern or not, the major critic of the previous generation, H. L. Mencken, was not impressed. He attacked the writing as:

"The sort of brave, bold stuff that all atheistic young newspaper reporters write. Jesus Christ in lower case. A hanging, carnal love, and two disembowelings."

But critic Edmund Wilson, a man of Hemingway's own generation, strongly disagreed:

"I am inclined to think that little book had more artistic dignity than anything else about the period of the war that had yet been written by an American."

These short sketches were intense, serious, and pared to the bone. They were like images slowly passing before the eye in a nightmare. They recreated the violence of our time like no other writing. Here's how Hemingway described the execution of six cabinet ministers in the aftermath of revolution:

"One of the ministers was sick with typhoid. Two soldiers carried him downstairs and out into the rain. They tried to hold him up against the wall but he sat down in a puddle of water. The other five stood very quietly against the wall. Finally the officer told the soldiers it was no good trying to make him stand up. When they fired the first volley he was sitting down in the water with his head on his knees."

Edmund Wilson lent the book to his old college chum, F. Scott Fitzgerald, who was suitably impressed:

# "He's the real thing."

Fitzgerald was an international celebrity. Only twenty-seven years old, he was already one of the highest paid writers in America. He had authored three novels, including the classic *The Great Gatsby*. Notorious for heavy drinking and wild exploits, Scott and his wife, Zelda, were often depicted in popular magazines as models for the "flaming youth" of the Jazz Age.

When Fitzgerald arrived in France, the person he most wanted to meet was Hemingway. They ran into each other at the Dingo Bar in Montmartre. Scott was not disappointed.

That first night, Fitzgerald passed out from drinking and had to be carried home. That's how the friendship began—with Ernest, the younger man, playing older brother. From the start it was a one-sided relationship.

**Say anything you please, but lay off Ernest.
—Scott**

Fitzgerald admired Hemingway's athletic physique, his interest in sports, and the way he could swill whiskey without losing control. Yet Scott's wife failed to share her husband's growing hero worship.

Zelda called Hemingway "bogus, as phony as a rubber check, a materialistic mystic," and "a pansy with hair on his chest." No one, she insisted, could be as male as all that. Even Hemingway's writing about Spain she denounced as nothing more than:

> Bullfighting, bullslinging, and bullsh...
> —Zelda

> I thought Zelda was crazy the first time I met her and you complicated it even more by being in love with her, and, of course you're a rummy.
> —Hemingway

In truth, Hemingway was a good deal more sensitive than he liked to pretend. And like Fitzgerald, he was definitely capable of falling under a woman's spell.

Duff Twysden, a tall, shapely woman in her early thirties had definitely caught Hemingway's eye. Duff wore her hair close cropped, bushed back like a boy—a style that would soon become a fashion. She had already been married twice, once to a titled British Lord.

Lady Duff was impressive. She had sophistication, she held a title, and she could hold her liquor. Hemingway was dazzled. But they probably never actually slept together. Duff had certain scruples, after all. She knew Ernest was married with a kid. And she genuinely liked Hadley. The fictional character Ernest later based on Duff expressed her unique sense of mortality in these terms:

"You know, it makes one feel rather good deciding not to be bitch. It's sort of what we hav instead of God."

Duff's charms were also not lost on a fellow writer by the name of Harold Loeb. He and Hem were friends. They used to box together and play tennis. Loeb, an American Jew from a wealthy family, was the far better player. He had money and graduated from an Ivy League college. But what probably irked Hemingway most of all was that Harold had already published a successful novel.

Loeb went off with Duff for a brief affair that ended just before Hemingway's annual pilgrimage to Spain. This time a whole mob was going down, including Hadley, Loeb, Duff, and the man she was currently engaged to, Pat Guthrie.

Down in Pamplona, drinks flowed and tempers flared. Loeb committed an unforgivable sin. He admitted to being bored by bullfighting.

Pat Guthrie noticed Loeb and Duff both suddenly disappearing one afternoon from a cafe. Next morning she showed up with a black eye. Loeb demanded to know why. There was an argument. Hemingway shouted that Loeb had already done enough to spoil the party.

Pat told Loeb to leave. He said he would, but only if Duff told him to go. She insisted that she definitely did not want him to go. Hemingway was furious:

"You lousy bastard.
Running to a woman."

Soon another woman appeared on the scene. Her name was Pauline Pfeiffer. She had none of Duff's scruples about married men.

Pauline however, worked for *Vogue* magazine as a fashion writer. She was trim and petite. She had stylishly short brown hair, and her family was one of the richest in the state of Arkansas.

Pauline's first impression of Hemingway was that he was a slovenly lout who dominated his wife and kept her in rags. This changed. Soon friends began to notice that Pauline was speaking in the spare, clipped phrases we today know as perfect "Hemingway."

When the family left Paris that winter to ski in Schruns, Switzerland, Pauline came for a long visit.

Ernest had just finished *The Torrents of Spring*, a mean-spirited parody of Sherwood Anderson's more simplistic writing.

Hemingway was tired of having people point out Anderson's influence on his writing. Hemingway wanted to be viewed as an original. And he hated being in anyone's debt — personal or professional. *Torrents* would drive a wedge between them once and for all. There was also business to consider. Anderson was responsible for getting Hemingway a contract with his publisher.

Scott Fitzgerald had landed Hemingway a much better deal from the influential firm of Scribners. Hemingway realized that Anderson's people would never print a book so harmful to the reputation of their star writer. They'd break the contract. And he could switch over to Scribners. Which is exactly what happened.

Hadley was upset that Ernest attacked an old friend like Anderson. Pauline disagreed. She thought *Torrents* a fine satire.

Hemingway had fallen in love. But his guilt made him feel as if he was in some private kind of hell:

## "With plenty of insomnia to light the way around so I could study the terrain."

He poured his anguish into a new book, *The Sun Also Rises*, about the whole expatriate scene in Paris and about bullfighting and love and honor and disillusionment.

Hemingway used the events of the previous summer to create the definitive portrait of what Gertrude Stein called "a lost generation"—young men and women whose values and morals had been shaped by the War.

These young people had lost their innocence. War had left them with a vast unconcern for the future and an enormous appetite for pleasure. Danger had made the experience of pleasure even sharper. For many, peacetime seemed like only an extended leave from the Front.

Hemingway caught all of this in his new book. He had changed the names of his friends and some of the details, but the real identities of the characters were obvious to anyone in Paris.

Duff is portrayed as Lady Brett, a young war widow trying to bury her loss with drink, sex, and adventure. Robert Cohen, the character based on Loeb, is made out to be a love struck fool, full of illusions. Most of the others try to stay drunk, live for the day and not risk any unnecessary consequences.

This solution is impossible for Jake Barnes, the Hemingway character. He is a war hero whose wounds have emasculated him. Jake is able to feel sexual desire, but not satisfy it. His love for Brett is hopeless. In the end, he sacrifices his dignity and self-respect in pursuit of her. But he learns to see beyond the last of his illusions.

Hemingway wanted to balance the deep pessimism that runs through the book with the following quote from the Bible. It summarized his basic philosophy in many ways. He believed that it helped to put the vanity of human affairs into perspective:

> "One generation passeth away, and another generation cometh; but the earth abideth forever."
>
> –Ecclesiastes

*The Sun Also Rises* was finished on April 1, 1926. That summer the Hemingways visited with the Fitzgeralds down in the south of France. Soon after, Pauline came to stay.

Hadley put up with things as best she could. It was now obvious that her husband was having as affair. More than once she broke down and had to be escorted home by friends.

At the end of the summer, the Hemingways traveled north to Paris together and once there, permanently moved into separate accommodations.

# TO HAVE AND HAVE NOT

There are only two kinds of tragedy, Oscar Wilde once wrote. The first is not getting what you want. And the other is getting it. Over the next decade, Hemingway would have plenty of chances to explore both kinds.

Hadley agreed to a divorce. But there was a catch. She insisted that Ernest and Pauline separate for 100 days. If they still loved each other, they could marry.

Pauline sailed to exile in America, while Hemingway stayed in Paris. When someone asked why he was leaving Hadley, he said:

"Because I am a son of a bitch."

Hadley took pity on him and agreed to a divorce before the 100 days were over. Hemingway tried to make amends by signing over the royalties from *The Sun Also Rises*.

The marriage was legally dissolved on January 27, 1927. But Pauline wanted to be wed within the Catholic Church, which does not recognize divorce. For Ernest to marry Pauline he would have to declare that his first marriage was illegitimate, a non-event. He agreed.

Catholicism attracted him. It was a key part of the Latin culture he loved. There was something ancient, elemental, even pagan about it—like bullfighting. Plus the Church's emphasis on Christ suffering on the cross and the martyred saints appealed to his pessimistic sense of realism. It was the best religion for a soldier. Besides, as Pauline pointed out:

"The outlet of confession would be very good for him."

Hemingway's second marriage eventually took place in May. Wedding gifts poured in from the far-flung Pfeiffer clan. Pauline's Uncle Gus paid for their comfortable Paris apartment and offered to buy them a home wherever they desired.

Ernest kept writing. His second collection of short fiction, *Men Without Women*, contained stories about bullfighters, jockeys, hired killers, corrupt prize fighters, and other hard-boiled types. But there were also a number of love stories—with unhappy endings.

Hemingway wasn't discouraged when several critics attacked his bleak vision of love and life. And he wasn't discouraged when Pauline told him that she was pregnant and wanted to have the baby in America. This time he had no complaints about leaving Europe. He knew he would be returning home a literary hero.

Besides, he was running out of friends in France. Many took Hadley's side in the divorce. Others resented the portrayals in *The Sun Also Rises*. Some objected to the way Ernest turned on the people who once had helped him. And a few—including Gertrude Stein—just seemed plain jealous of his success.

Success did seem to have changed him. "You were not to disagree with the Master in any way from then on," recalled writer Donald Ogden Stewart, a friend from the Paris days. If you did, Ernest regarded it as a breech of trust.

If you crossed Hemingway, you could never be sure when he'd turn on you. The man could be so nice that his mean streak startled you. Maybe it was more of a mood thing, something chemical. Maybe it was the heavy drinking. In any case, Ernest was becoming a dangerous pal to have.

Novelist John Dos Passos was one of Hemingway's last literary friends. He was hard at work on an epic trilogy of American life called *U.S.A.*

It was Dos who told him about Key West, an island at the southern tip of Florida that he'd come across in his many travels. Key West was just one and a half miles wide, four and a half miles long. Accessible only by ferry, the island was 120 miles from the American mainland and only 90 miles from Havana, Cuba.

The population of 10,000 was made up of Cubans, blacks, and conchs—the descendants of Yankee whalers. The unpainted frame houses on the tree–lined streets actually had a New England look to them. But the rest was strictly tropical.

"It's the best place I've ever been any time anywhere, flowers, tamarind trees, guava trees, coconut palms."

The Hemingways arrived in April of 1928. A brand new yellow Ford was waiting when they got off the boat from France—yet another gift from Uncle Gus. Ernest quickly settled in. He liked the rundown, unpretentious look of the town, which he called the "Saint Tropez of the Poor."

He wrote four or five hours in the morning while it was still cool. Then he was free to have a drink, a swim, or to hang out with the new friends he'd made:

Charles Thompson, an easy going, well-educated young man of 30, whose family owned a number of local businesses;

Captain Bra Saunders, the experienced skipper of a deep sea charter boat;

and Joe Russell, an avid angler, and sometime smuggler, who also happened to own Ernest's favorite dive—a saloon known as Sloppy Joe's.

What these men had in common was a taste for fishing and drinking. In their company, Hemingway felt like a kid again:

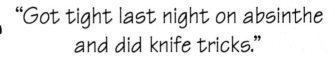

"Got tight last night on absinthe and did knife tricks."

Pauline figured on sailing back to Europe as soon as the baby was born, but Ernest insisted that they try to find a house in Key West—one big enough for a new addition to the family.

Patrick Hemingway was born on June 28, 1928, after a difficult, dangerous birth. Ernest left the screaming baby and Pauline with her family, while he took off to Wyoming to escape the summer heat, to hunt and to write. Neither parent liked little kids much, and soon Pauline was planning to join her husband.

She had learned from Hadley's mistake. Pauline would never let children get in the way of her marriage to Ernest.

In December he traveled to New York to meet his oldest son, Bumby, who had sailed over from France. On the train he received a telegram announcing the death of his father. Ernest engaged a porter to take Bumby on to Florida. Then, he hurried west to Chicago.

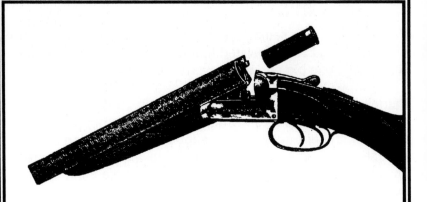

Dr. Hemingway had shot himself in the head with his father's ancient Civil War revolver. He'd been depressed about bad investments, debts, and his diabetic condition. He feared, probably incorrectly, that one of his legs would have to be amputated.

At the funeral, Ernest told his kid brother, Leicester, that the doctor's suicide was not a sin. Father was obviously out of his head. But Hemingway enraged his older sister, Marcelline, by saying that his Catholic beliefs had taught him that suicides rot in hell.

Ernest was deeply wounded by his father's suicide. He tried to bury his hurt by working hard on a new book that he would call *A Farewell to Arms*.

The novel was about a young American, badly wounded in battle, serving in the Italian Army. A beautiful British nurse bathes him, mothers him, and eventually makes love to him in his hospital bed. The young man returns to the Front and is almost killed during a disastrous retreat. He, then, decides to escape with his lover to neutral Switzerland. There she tragically dies in childbirth.

# A FAREWELL TO ARMS

The hero is devastated. Life seems to him a brutal game with no winners. The best you could do was to try to gain the maximum rewards from the game: honor, dignity, and the pleasures of playing:

"You did not know what it was about. You never had time to learn. They threw you in and told you the rules and the first time they caught you off base they killed you."

Hemingway tried thirty-two different endings before he got the precise mix of sex and doom that expressed his deepest feelings.

*A Farewell to Arms* was published in the fall of 1929. It sold 50,000 copies in the first month, despite the great Wall Street "crash."

Dorothy Parker's profile of the author soon after marks the first flowering of the Hemingway myth. Ms. Parker compared her respect for his talent and integrity to the awe a tourist might feel viewing the Grand Canyon at sunset. She also introduced the American public to Hemingway's own definition of courage, namely: "Grace under pressure."

At that moment Ernest was feeling pressure from another Grace—his mother. He had assumed the role of the man of the family. Every month he sent money home. But now Grace Hemingway stubbornly refused to follow his financial advice:

" Never threaten me with what to do. Your father tried that once when we were first married and lived to regret it."

–Grace

My *dear mother,* I am a very different man from my father.

In years to come, Hemingway would strive to prove that fact. If Ed had died a coward by his own hand, Ernie would show them all how to be a hero.

# DEATH IN THE AFTERNOON

This rebellion led him to write his first nonfiction book, *Death in the Afternoon*. Only in the bullfight arena could he study the mystery of death with his eyes wide open. But there was more than death on his mind. The matador was not a butcher. He was an artist.

"When a man is still in rebellion against death he had pleasure in taking to himself one of the Godlike attributes; that of giving it."

The matador defies death. And he shares this feeling with all who watch. That is his art.

"It is impossible to believe the emotional and spiritual intensity and pure, classic beauty that can be produced by a man, an animal and a piece of scarlet serge draped over a stick."

People die and civilizations crumble. But good writing endures, because it is able to evoke emotion in any one who reads it. Literature, for Hemingway, was a sensation machine that he hoped would ensure his immortality.

But Hemingway was not content to pick away at the reader's sense of propriety with shocking details and occasional vulgarity. He also tried to sink his sword into the reputation of writers such as George Orwell, Jean Cocteau, and William Faulkner. No living writer was fit to stand with him in the arena of literature.

Socialist writer, Max Eastman, wondered why Ernest was swaggering around "roaring about whorehouses and bulls blood"? Was there something in his background that made him want to prove time and again that he had real hair on his chest?

This struck a nerve. But for the moment, Ernest tried to forget all the criticism with a frenzy of...

Fishing. Setting records for the biggest sailfish caught, the biggest tuna, the biggest marlin. And then breaking them one by one.

Hunting. Covering his home with trophy heads and skins from summers out West.

And drinking. He was now calling alcohol the "Giant Killer."

His next conquest was the beautiful wife of an American millionaire living in Cuba: Jane Mason.

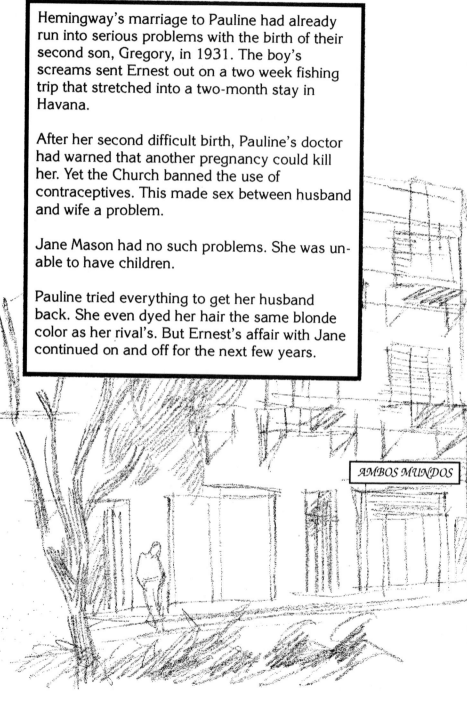

Hemingway's marriage to Pauline had already run into serious problems with the birth of their second son, Gregory, in 1931. The boy's screams sent Ernest out on a two week fishing trip that stretched into a two-month stay in Havana.

After her second difficult birth, Pauline's doctor had warned that another pregnancy could kill her. Yet the Church banned the use of contraceptives. This made sex between husband and wife a problem.

Jane Mason had no such problems. She was unable to have children.

Pauline tried everything to get her husband back. She even dyed her hair the same blonde color as her rival's. But Ernest's affair with Jane continued on and off for the next few years.

AMBOS MUNDOS

Hemingway now rushed to get a new collection of stories into print. It was called *Winner Take Nothing*, a title which expressed his growing sense of futility. War, murder, madness, suicide, castration, natural disaster, divorce, accidents, and illness were the topics he chose to write about.

His tragic view was brilliantly captured in the story, "A Clean Well-Lighted Place." Here a waiter at a late-night cafe sympathizes with a dignified old man who had recently tried to kill himself.

What did he fear? It was not fear or dread. It was emptiness. A sense of nothingness he knew too well. Some lived in it and never felt it, but he felt it . And he knew it was all *nada*—the Spanish word for nothing. All a person can do is to outlast the night until it is safe to sleep. There's no other way. For in the end, even salvation has been reduced to a mocking litany of *nada*:

"Hail nothing full of
nothing,
nothing is with thee."

The collection was uneven. Some of Hemingway's best writing alternated with thin sketches and even an essay lifted right out of *Death in the Afternoon*. Again reviews were poor. But what hurt most was an unexpected attack from his old mentor, Gertrude Stein, who said Hemingway had a great story to tell— if he only had the courage to tell it.

Ernest tried to forget by going off by himself on an adventure for which he'd waited a lifetime: an African safari. Pauline's Uncle Gus would pay for everything. Charles Thompson, Ernie's Key West buddy, agreed to come along. To lead the expedition they hired "white hunter" Phillip Percival. He was the same handsome, dashing Englishman who had served Theodore Roosevelt twenty years before.

Little wonder that Hemingway had a sheepish grin plastered over his face at first. But as the trophies began to mount up there was trouble.

In just the first two weeks, the expedition bagged lions, leopards, hyenas, and the full limit on cheetahs, gazelles, antelopes, and other animals. But Charles Thompson seemed to be getting all the finest heads. Hemingway began to seethe with envy.

"We have very primitive emotions...
It's impossible not to be competitive.
Spoils everything though."

—Hemingway

# THE PILAR

On his return to America, Hemingway the man heated up his competition with the Hemingway the myth. He signed a contract with *Esquire* magazine to write a series of "letters," mostly on sporting themes. These pieces were written in the first person and concerned the exploits and opinions of a world-class sportsman and celebrity. A hefty advance let him buy an expensive motor yacht he dubbed, the *Pilar*, which quickly became the seagoing extension of Hemingway's new identity. He now began calling himself Papa. And he made sure there were always plenty of people around to watch his exploits. More than ever, he hated to be alone.

*The Green Hills of Africa* was supposed to be an "absolutely true" nonfiction record of his safari. But the book had an even worse reception than *Death in the Afternoon*. Critic Edmund Wilson, an early Hemingway fan, claimed that Ernest wrote what must be one of the only books which make Africa and its animals seem dull.

"Almost the only thing we learn about the animals is that Hemingway wants to kill them."

Worse, all we learn about the Africans is that they are childlike and that they worship the worthy author. Ernest Hemingway, Wilson concludes, is certainly the worst character he ever created.

Fortunately, the Old Master usually saved the best material for his fiction. The story called "The Snows of Kilimanjaro" is a rare work of technical mastery, imagination, and confession. It was written a year after the non-fiction Africa book. And it was absolutely true—even if it was invented.

A rich American writer is slowly dying of gangrene out in the African bush. His wife has Pauline's talent for self-sacrifice and Jane Mason's good looks. She is desperately trying to keep her husband alive long enough for help to arrive.

"He had destroyed his talent by not using it, by betrayals of himself and what he believed in, by drinking so much that it blunted the edge of perceptions, by laziness, by sloth, and by snobbery, by pride and by prejudice, by hook or crook."

He blamed the rich who were dull and drank too much. He blamed his wife who tried to make things too soft for him. And he blamed himself for trading in on his talent and vitality. Now all that was coming to an end.

The writer is loaded on a small plane. The earth suddenly shrinks away. Up ahead is the high snowy peak of Kilimanjaro, shining unbelievably white in the sun. That's where he thinks he is going.

Hemingway then shatters this illusion. The scene shifts suddenly. The writer's wife awakens to the sound of a hyena prowling around the camp. She finds her husband dead. And that is the only truth we are left with.

Papa had now become his own enemy. To demonstrate "grace under pressure," you need pressure. If the world won't supply it, you must manufacture it yourself. Or else go slack.

Papa's belly now bulged over his waistband. The drinks kept flowing. He continued to hunt. He now boxed with the local black men who "went easy on him" for fifty cents a round. And he kept fishing, sometimes for months at a time. But nothing mattered anymore.

**"I felt that giant bloody emptiness and nothingness."**

Hemingway confessed to John Dos Passos that he feared he would never make love again, never fight, never write. He had everything, and all on his own terms. And he was now all for death.

# THE SPANISH EARTH

In the fall of 1935, a powerful hurricane struck southern Florida. Nearly 1,000 jobless World War I veterans were trapped at a federal work camp on an unprotected key. The Government failed to evacuate the men in time. When disaster struck, a wall of water 20 feet high rolled over the island, driven by 150 mile per hour winds.

Hemingway took the *Pilar* out five times to hunt for survivors. All he saw were the dead:

> "You found them everywhere and in the sun all of them were beginning to be too big for their blue jeans and jackets that they could never fill when they were on the bum and hungry."

Sickened, he wrote an indictment of the US government, published in the Socialist magazine, *The New Masses*. The article was called "Who Killed the Vets." It was the first time in years that Hemingway's sense of injustice extended to anything outside of himself.

Most people couldn't understand this sudden rebirth of conscience. Throughout the Great Depression hard times of the 1930s, Hemingway seemed unconcerned and self-indulgent.

What did Hemingway have to write about anymore that anyone wanted to read?

His most recent published fiction was a long short story which would eventually grow into the novel called *To Have and Have Not*. Gritty and well written, it was also relentlessly depressing. The story introduced America to one of Hemingway's least attractive heroes: Harry Morgan, an inarticulate loner with the same name as a notorious Caribbean pirate. He doesn't let too much thought get in the way of action.

Harry cares only about his independence, his boat, and feeding his family. Harry gets involved with smuggling when a rich sports-man cheats him out of his fee. But the deal goes sour. Harry winds up snapping the neck of an unarmed man and tosses the body overboard. The following night he's still able to sit contentedly in his living room, listening to the radio, a cool drink in his hand.

Hemingway's rage over the dead vets was soon turned back against himself. Now it was his own death that stared him in the face:

"Me, I like life very much. So much it will be a big disgust when I have to shoot myself. Maybe pretty soon I guess although will arrange to be shot in order not to have a bad effect on the kids."

This would not be necessary. In July 1936, war broke out in Spain. General Francisco Franco and a junta of high military officers tried to overthrow the freely elected government.

Maybe Hemingway would find a reason to live by going to cover the war. Or maybe he could find a way to die. Either way, he knew he had to go.

And soon he had a pretty young woman to accompany him. Her name was Martha Gellhorn. She was a talented writer with two books to her name. She also happened to be 28 years old, blonde, and shapely.

Martha came to Key West to meet Hemingway. The young admirer saw a great deal of the Old Master. Within a few days she was calling him "Ernestino." Pauline was jealous of this new rival, but there was little she could do.

Early in 1937, Hemingway slipped into Spain from neutral France. Martha joined him a month later. By this time, Ernest had shifted from a neutral correspondent of a large American news syndicate to an impassioned partisan in Spain. For him the lines were sharply drawn.

On the Right was General Franco and the Spanish Army allied with the Catholic Church, the rich, and the fascistic blue shirts of the Falange Movement. And they were supported by the armed might of Mussolini's Italy and Hitler's Germany.

Opposing them were the people of Spain—landless farmers, workers with nothing to lose and those in the middle class who still believed in freedom.

Political parties of the Center and Left stopped bickering long enough to form a shaky Popular Front government. For Hemingway:

> "...my sympathies are always for exploited working people against absentee landlords even if I drink around with landlords and shoot pigeons with them. I would just as soon shoot them as pigeons."

Thousands of working people came to the defense of the Republic. They seized weapons and manned the trenches circling Madrid, the capital. Franco's forces were stopped dead. When Hemingway moved into his room at the Hotel Florida, the fighting was still going on only 17 blocks away.

His Spanish friends were happy to see a writer of Hemingway's stature committed to their cause. They eagerly supplied him with a car, a driver, and precious gasoline in order to cover the action.

Hem trudged behind the infantry with a movie camera on his shoulder, filming the government tanks "as they moved like ships up the steep hills and deployed into action."

This striking war footage was later assembled by director Joris Ivens to make the influential documentary called *The Spanish Earth.*

At the Front, Hemingway stayed cool under fire. It wasn't hard. He wasn't afraid of dying. He was afraid of living. And being afraid.

"In Spain I had no fear after a couple weeks and was very happy."

Martha shared his hotel room, which he somehow managed to stock with food, coffee, and cases of scotch. The place soon became an unofficial headquarters for journalists from around the world. Martha, too, was writing articles for American magazines. She learned Spanish, visited hospitals and crowded city morgues, and endured the constant bombardment all around her. They were happy. And why not?

"It was the one time in his life
when he wasn't the most important thing around."

Hemingway now began to describe his commitment to the Republic in religious terms. He said it was like feeling the way a person expected to feel—but did not—when making First Communion.

At night, Ernest wrote articles and helped Martha edit her work. And after several months at war, she accompanied him home to America. Hemingway returned alone to Key West. He and Pauline made a pretense of getting along while he finished writing *To Have and Have Not.*

The theme of the book was evolving. He began writing new episodes that showed Harry Morgan destroyed by an uncaring world around him.

Hem also wrote the narration for *The Spanish Earth* and accompanied the documentary around the country, drumming up support for Spain. Enough money was donated to send off dozens of ambulances to the beleaguered Republic.

Scott Fitzgerald attended a fundraiser in Hollywood, where he now worked as a screenwriter. His friendship with Hemingway had suffered over the years. Ernest had hurt Scott by criticizing his writing, his intellect, his personal courage, and even his wife Zelda, who was in a mental institution. Yet Fitzgerald now saw Hemingway in a new light:

"Ernest came like a whirlwind. I feel he was in a state of nervous intensity, that there was something almost religious about it."

Hemingway had become a believer. He went on to give one of the few speeches of his life at an important conference of American writers. "Fascism," he told the crowd, " is a lie told by bullies." It was not enough to worry about Hitler and Mussolini. People must fight, for some things are even worse than war.

President Franklin Roosevelt invited Ernest and Martha to the White House to show the documentary. FDR was impressed. Yet America, like Britain and France, remained neutral. So while Mussolini's submarines sank unarmed Republican tankers on the high seas and Hitler's planes bombed defense-less civilians in the hill town of Guernica—the western democracies did nothing.

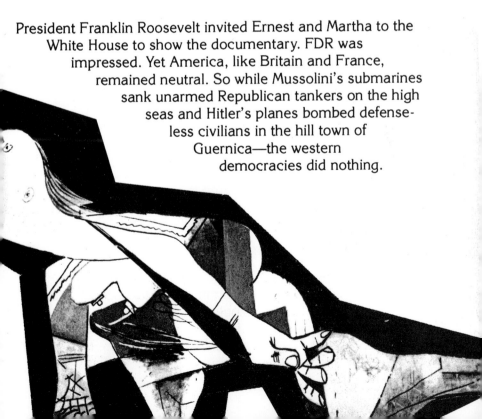

Back in Madrid, Hemingway wrote his only play, *The Fifth Column*. While he worked, his hotel was hit more than 30 times by enemy high explosive shells.

> "So if it is not a good play,
> perhaps that is what is the matter with it."

The play was about a hard-boiled American working with Spanish counter–intelligence and a beautiful blonde reporter with "the loveliest damn body in the world." Their names were Philip Rawlings and Dorothy Bridges. Any resemblance to Ernesto and Marty was far from accidental.

The Republic was slowly bleeding to death. Its people were close to starvation. A naval blockade by the "neutral" nations had cut off all supplies.

After a last desperate assault on Franco's forces, the Republican army started to collapse. The assault left Hemingway and a team of reporters trapped on the wrong side of the Ebro. They found a rowboat to take them to safety. But the current soon dragged them toward some "nasty rapids." Ernest took the oars and somehow got the boat to safety.

For Spain he could do no more. In March of 1939, Franco's troops goose–stepped into Madrid. Six months later, as Hemingway correctly predicted, World War II began.

By this time, Hemingway was living openly with Martha Gellhorn in Cuba. He was writing better than he had in a decade. A new novel was emerging from his experience. It was a story which would make the struggle in Spain come alive for millions of readers just waking up to the threat of war and world tyranny. And it began with these words from poet John Donne:

"No man is an Iland, intire of it self..."

# MEN AT WAR

For Whom the Bell Tolls summed up everything Hemingway had learned about Spain and war, life and death, courage and cowardice. With the defeat of the Republic he felt free to tell the whole story—without sparing anyone. The words practically flooded out of him.

The plot was deceptively simple. An American volunteer named Robert Jordan is ordered to blow up a bridge behind the Fascist lines. This mission is linked to a major Republican offensive. But the Spanish leaders are incompetent, and their Soviet allies unscrupulous. Jordan suspects that the offensive is doomed before it starts. Yet he cannot back out.

In the mountains he links up with a guerrilla band led by an indomitable Gypsy woman and her cowardly husband. And for the first time, he falls in love. She is a beautiful young woman called Maria, whose hair was cropped by the Fascist troops who brutally raped her.

Facing death Jordan's emotions are magnified, sharpened. There's meaning in everything. He feels closer to the earth and the sky than ever before. And love is all that matters. For as he confesses to Maria:

"Thou art me now too.
Thou art all that will be of me."

The book was published in October of 1940. Within six months, it had sold a remarkable half-million copies. Hemingway was delighted to be back on top again:

"Book selling like frozen Daiquiris in hell."

Hemingway and Martha were now living at the *Finca,* a rundown estate in the Cuban countryside, surrounded by twenty acres of tropical foliage. Hemingway wanted to get remarried immediately. He explained to Martha that it would make life simpler. She had her doubts:

"Myself, I think living in sin is wonderful."

Martha wasn't content simply being Mrs. Hemingway. She desperately wanted to resume her own career as a journalist. So she sailed alone to Finland to cover that country's winter war with Russia. Hemingway was miserable:

"I need a wife in bed
and not in the most widely circulated magazines."

Ernest reluctantly agreed to accompany Martha on her next assignment to Asia. Both would report on the growing threat of war with Japan. The couple covered 13,000 miles under the worst possible conditions.

FINCA VIGIA

Back in Cuba, Hemingway now worried if he could ever top the success of *For Whom the Bell Tolls*. When writing became too difficult, there were always the pleasures of Havana to distract him. For a while at least.

On December 7, 1941, the Japanese attacked Pearl Harbor. Martha couldn't wait to cover the fighting overseas. But Papa had other ideas.

He got US government approval to organize a volunteer counter–intelligence operation in Havana. There were 300,000 Spaniards living in Cuba. Some of them were Franco supporters who just might help the German U-boats now operating freely through the Caribbean. The Crook Factory was the name Hemingway gave to his spy network. There were nearly thirty agents in the group, most of them needy exiles from Republican Spain. Ernest, naturally, was Numero Uno. Unfortunately, the Crook Factory obtained little hard intelligence.

Next Hemingway talked the US Ambassador in Havana into turning the *Pilar* into an anti-submarine hunter. It was equipped with machine guns, explosives, and even a bazooka and manned by Ernest's friends: rich athletes, fishermen, a radical priest, and even a jai alai player.

The men on board spent months at sea fishing, drinking, and lobbing the occasional grenade into the water when things grew too dull. Martha was angered and embarrassed by Papa's "disgraceful playacting." She had seen the real face of war in Italy and North Africa. And where was the great Ernest Hemingway? The couple's quarrels turned bitter:

"He woke me when I was trying to sleep to bully, snarl, mock—my crime was really to have been at war when he was not."

Hemingway was eventually shamed into action. He made a deal with Martha's publisher and got the correspondent's credentials that she had counted on. Then he pulled strings and got a seat on a plane over to England. He claimed that was too dangerous for a woman. So Martha wound up sailin the sub–infested waters of the Atlantic in a slow boat loade with high explosives.

Meanwhile, Ernest lived it up. He roomed at the posh Dorchester hotel, stayed stewed and swaggered around London in his US Army correspondent's uniform. And he even met a woman.

Mary Welsh was an American reporter, 36, blond, petite and shapely. Hemingway immediately pursued her. He followed her up to her room and told her that although he didn't know her—he would someday marry her.

"I'm a fool with women—I always marry them."

Soon after, Hemingway suffered his first injury of the war. He was being driven home from a drunken revel through the blacked-out streets when his car crashed. He was still in the hospital, his head turbaned in bandages, on the day that Martha finally arrived in England.

Hemingway knew well that alcohol made head wounds worse. Yet there were plenty of empty bottles under his bed. Martha was furious. She had plenty of time to think during the long voyage across the Atlantic. Ernest's drunken, "ceaseless, crazy bullying" had gone too far. The third Mrs. Hemingway told her husband that they were through:

"I loved him as long as I could and when I lost all respect for him—as a man—not as a writer— I said so and withdrew and that was that."

—Martha Gellhorn

On June 6, 1944, Ernest crossed the English Channel in a small landing ship headed for the beaches of Normandy. But his head injury kept him out of action. On the evening of D-Day he was back in London, writing an article called "How We Took Fox Green Beach."

Yet that didn't stop other reporters from filing stories about the exploits of this Hemingway guy who led the troops up the beaches and onward to victory. The myth had already overtaken the man.

We have a jolly and gay life, full of deeds, German loot, much shooting, much fightin

Soon Hemingway suffered an even more serious concussion. He had been out riding through the French countryside on a motorcycle with famous photographer Robert Capa. They were trying to locate enemy positions when they ran into a German anti-tank gun dug in beside the road. At the last moment, Ernest flipped the cycle and dove into a ditch. He lay there motionless for several hours until the enemy at last moved off.

The fall damaged his head and liver, and worst of all, left him impotent.

This didn't stop him from setting up his own private army. Task Force Hem was made up of French Resistance fighters Ernest had recruited. And his mission was to collect intelligence about Nazi positions on the road into the occupied French capital.

When it was time to advance, Hemingway led his Resistance fighters into the embattled city of Paris. The Task Force paused to clear some snipers out of the Bois de Boulogne. Then the *Capitain* moved on to liberate the wine cellar at the Ritz Hotel.

It was at the Ritz that Mary Welsh finally caught up with him. Liberated Paris was for lovers, and they were no exception. Mary patiently overcame Ernest's impotence by treating him "as the hotshot warrior, macho man, great in bed." Hemingway was more than grateful:

"Could you be my Pickle? Sour but pungent?"

Their relationship was sweet and sour from the first. When drunk, he attacked her as a "goddamn smirking, useless female correspondent." He compared her to a black widow spider. He fired six bullets into a photo of Mary's former husband. And once—when she complained about his intoxicated Army buddies—he even slapped her.

"You poor coward. You poor, fat featherheaded coward. You woman-hitter."
—Mary Welsh

Hemingway joined the American Fourth Infantry Division just in time for some of the most brutal fighting of the war. At first Hemingway reveled in the "fear-purged, purging ecstasy of battle." But not for long. As he began to see his friends die one by one, the carnage began to take its emotional toll.

Towards the end of a month-long battle near the German border, Hemingway sent a crazed poem to Mary that seemed to capture the fragmentary unreality of combat:

Now sleeps he with that old whore Death.
Who yesterday denied her twice.
Repeat after me.
Did you deny her?
Yes.
Thrice?
Yes...
Make feet move on slowly now
Make feet follow where no plow
Leads you ahead
Where things are sown
To the place where you'll be dead...
Throw your love away
You must do it slowly now.
Slow now and pray
Pray to all of nothing
Pray to all of nil
Throw away your own true love
Walking up a hill.

In March of 1945, the Germans were close to surrender. Hemingway's war had come to an end. He was returning to Cuba, where Mary would soon wed him. In the future, Ernest's final battles would be with himself alone.

In Havana, he returned to his old pleasures, but peace was hell. Hemingway's heavy drinking seemed out of control. An old Army buddy, General "Buck" Lanaham, visited Hem in 1949. He estimated that Ernie was polishing off nearly two quarts of booze per diem. He took sleeping pills on top of all the alcohol and still rose at dawn to write.

> "Before he wrote a book he'd go into training.
> That is, he wouldn't take a drink before noon."
> —Lanaham

Hemingway was trying to write—with mixed results. He abandoned a large novel about the Caribbean, which was later edited by Mary and published posthumously as *Islands in the Stream*. It was heavily autobiographical, with his old friend Marlene Dietrich as the main love interest. And it ended with a romantic war fantasy about hunting down German U-boats. Here the mythic Hemingway seemed to reign supreme.

But, another Hemingway came alive in his intriguing unfinished novel, *The Garden of Eden*. It, too, was published after his death—and for good reason. The novel revealed sides of the author's inner life that he was struggling to understand, sides he had tried to conceal throughout his career.

*The Garden* begins with writer David Bourne and his wife Catherine honeymooning in the south of France. In no time, the couple have cut their hair identical lengths, dyed it the same color, and have been mistaken for brother and sister. They have also begun to engage in strange, androgynous sex play. Catherine declared to her husband:

> "You are changing. Oh you are. You are.
> Yes you are and you're my girl Catherine."

*The Garden of Eden* cast a powerful spell over Hemingway. While writing it he actually dyed his own hair a bright copper color. Yet he could never solve the technical problems of telling the story. And perhaps he was also afraid of unleashing his personal devils on the unsuspecting world.

Whatever his reasons, by 1950 he had failed to publish a major work of fiction in almost a decade, and it began to bother him.

"If I cannot work I usually do something bad and have remorse and then my conscience makes me work."

It was usually Mary who was on the receiving end of his frustration. She nursed her husband's frequent injuries and was in charge of his fragile ego.

But Mary couldn't offer the intellectual stimulation required, especially in the isolation of Cuba. Ernest began to feel he needed another kind of inspiration to write the next big book.

Adriana Ivancich was a pretty 18-year-old girl Ernest met on vacation in Venice. She was the youngest child of an impoverished aristocratic Italian family. When she offhandedly asked Hemingway to borrow a comb for her long dark hair, he broke his own in two pieces. The moment she took that offering, Ernest fell hopelessly in love.

The girl was impressed with the famous writer. But the elderly-looking man with thinning gray hair brushed forward like a Roman senator held no physical attraction for her. So the affair remained platonic. This romance was the basis for his next published novel.

*Across the River and Through the Trees* told of an aging US Army officer who'd been unfairly demoted during the War. To make matters worse, he suffers from a fatal heart condition. His desperate romance with a young Venetian girl is a last, reckless assertion of life in the face of death.

Hemingway invited Adriana to Cuba, accompanied by her mother. The girl's exotic good looks and sense of refinement made him even more frustrated with his wife. Ernest openly tried to drive Mary away.

Ernest was aware that he was making a fool of himself with the girl. Adriana soon found a young man her age in Havana. Yet Hemingway could not stop loving her, and the lost youth she represented.

When Adriana was returning to Italy, Ernest said he felt as if part of him was being amputated. The last time he saw her he wept like a baby:

"Look, daughter, look. Now you can tell everyone that you have seen Ernest Hemingway cry."

# THE UNDISCOVERED COUNTRY

He was still world champ. In the boxing terms he liked to use, he had gone the distance with most of the literary greats of the past. Yet the fact was that Ernest Hemingway had coasted on his reputation for a decade. Soon he would suffer his deepest personal misery in the midst of his greatest public triumph.

*Across the River and Through the Trees* was published in the fall of 1950. The reviews all seemed to agree it was the worst book of Hemingway's career. Delmore Schwartz, a poet and perceptive critic, summed up the general feeling about the novel with these words:

"Extremely bad in an ominous way."

Was he finished as a writer and a man? A profile of the author in the *New Yorker* magazine made that possibility seem likely. Journalist Lillian Ross interviewed Hemingway over the course of a long weekend. He had come to New York to deliver a manuscript and to do a little celebrating. Her article showed a man awash in a sea of alcohol.

Papa drank all day. He bragged, blustered, and beat his chest. He serenaded Ross with old Army songs, and kept repeating meaningless statements such as:

"How do you like it now, gentlemen."

Many readers wondered if Papa hadn't taken too many shots to the head.

Years later Gregory Hemingway recalled that the profile of Papa was "unintentionally devastating because it showed him exactly as he was at that time." But then, Gregory had a reason to be bitter.

As an unhappy eighteen–year–old, Gregory dropped out of school, moved to California, became involved with drugs and was arrested. Pauline called Papa long distance with the bad news. They quarreled. That night Pauline had a stroke, went into shock and died.

Ernest later accused Gregory to his face of killing his mother. It took the boy nearly a decade to recover. He eventually became a medical student and learned that the real cause of Pauline's death was a glandular tumor that affected her blood pressure when upset. Papa was as much to blame as anyone—or no one.

Hemingway was now only in his early 50s, although he looked fifteen years older. He knew he'd lost his "title" with *Across the River*. But he refused to hang up the gloves. Instead he channeled his sense of loss, the sense of his own limits and vulnerability, into a new book. Its hero had also seen better days.

*The Old Man and the Sea* was a story Hemingway had wanted to write for twenty years. It was about Santiago, an aging Cuban fisherman who'd gone 84 days without catching a single fish. Like Papa, he refused to surrender to his fate, declaring, "A man can be destroyed but not defeated." In desperation, the fisherman sails his boat far out into the Gulf Stream. Then he lowers his line far too deep into the blue waters.

Santiago hooks a giant marlin who tugs him even further out to sea. The life and death struggle goes on day and night. Like the matador who must make a pact with death in order to defy it, the fisherman himself is caught:

"You are killing me fish...But you have a right to. Never have I seen a greater, or more beautiful, a calmer or more noble thing than you, brother. Come on and kill me. I do not care who kills who."

The novel was published in a special edition of *Life* magazine. Over 5 million copies were sold during one week in September of 1952.

Hollywood wanted to make a movie out of the *Old Man*. And in 1953, the Pulitzer Prize Committee selected it as the book of the year. Papa was back.

144

That fall he returned to Africa with Mary and a rich Cuban friend. Papa was drinking so heavily that he fell out of a moving Land Rover. And his shooting was off. Embarrassed, he tried to take credit for someone else's kill.

He tried going native for a while. He shaved his head, dyed his clothes like a Massai warrior, and tried to go hunting with a spear. He even flirted with a young African girl—and later claimed she bore him a son.

A small Cessna airplane was hired to take the Hemingways over spectacular Murchison Falls, in Uganda. The plane suddenly dove to avoid a flock of birds, hit a telegraph wire, and crashed into the bush. Mary suffered two broken ribs, Ernest hurt his shoulder. That night they slept out in the forest around a fire, surrounded by a herd of elephants.

But someone had spotted the wrecked plane from the air, and millions around the world read the news that Ernest Hemingway was dead. Unfortunately, this is almost what happened the following day.

A second plane was hired to take the Hemingways to the hospital. Yet just a moment after take-off, the fuel tank aboard exploded into flames.

"Miss Mary had never seen a plane burn up. That's an impressive sight—especially when you're in the plane."

Ernest used his head to butt the door open. He escaped, but suffered yet another concussion. Brain fluid leaked from his skull. A vertebrae in his lower back was crushed painfully. He was vomiting and seeing double. There was damage to his head, liver, spleen, and kidneys.

Still, he was able to attend a press conference soon after in Entebbe. Reporters claimed that Hemingway arrived holding a bunch of bananas in one hand and a bottle of gin in the other.

The reality was far less glorious. Hemingway suffered yet another set of injuries while needlessly trying to put out a brush fire near camp. He suddenly lost balance and fell into the flames. His hair, lips, chest, and limbs were all badly scorched. When newsmen now tried to photograph him, Ernest angrily sent them away:

"It's not legal to surprise a defeated man."

146

Defeated? After Africa Hemingway did seem to change. To his friend Aaron Hotchner, Ernest seemed strangely diminished.

Defeated? For all the world, Papa was about to be awarded his greatest triumph. In October 1954, Hemingway received the Nobel Prize in literature for his "powerful, style-making mastery of the art of modern narration."

Ernest claimed he was still too weak to accept the award in person. So he sent a message which was delivered by the American ambassador to Sweden. It was uncharacteristically modest and mentioned several writers more deserving than he. And its description of the writer's life was especially moving:

"He grows in public stature as he sheds his loneliness and often his work deteriorates. For he does his work alone, and if he is a good enough writer he must face eternity, or the lack of it, each day."

Hemingway's powers of recuperation were failing for the first time in his life. Writing had become an ordeal. He tried working on *The Garden of Eden* again and had to give up. Then unexpectedly out of the past he received a rich literary legacy.

In 1956, the Ritz Hotel in Paris sent two dusty trunks they had found in their storeroom which included journals Ernest kept in the 1920s. Hemingway eagerly returned to the days when he was still young and had everything to learn.

**"If you are lucky enough to have lived in Paris as a young man, then wherever you go for the rest of your life, it stays with you, for Paris is a moveable feast."**

*A Moveable Feast* captures the part of a city that a man can only know on foot, know with his eyes and the touch of his hand, know through the hunger for food or work or recognition.

But the people fare poorly. Hemingway was viewing the past through the lens of memory. And that lens had been polished for 30 years by a master story teller with an ax to grind—not an historian.

Ford Maddox Ford is portrayed as a disgusting bumbler with social pretensions, bad breath, and grease stains on his clothes. Gertrude Stein is a lazy egoist sexually enthralled by Alice Toklas, who needed young Hemingway to teach her to write dialogue. "Poor" Scott Fitzgerald comes across as effeminate, henpecked to death, and convinced that his sexual organs were too small to satisfy.

He could never finish *A Moveable Feast*. It was edited by Mary and published posthumously. The last thing Hemingway ever lived to publish was an article in *Life* magazine about bullfighting. It was called, appropriately enough, *The Dangerous Summer*.

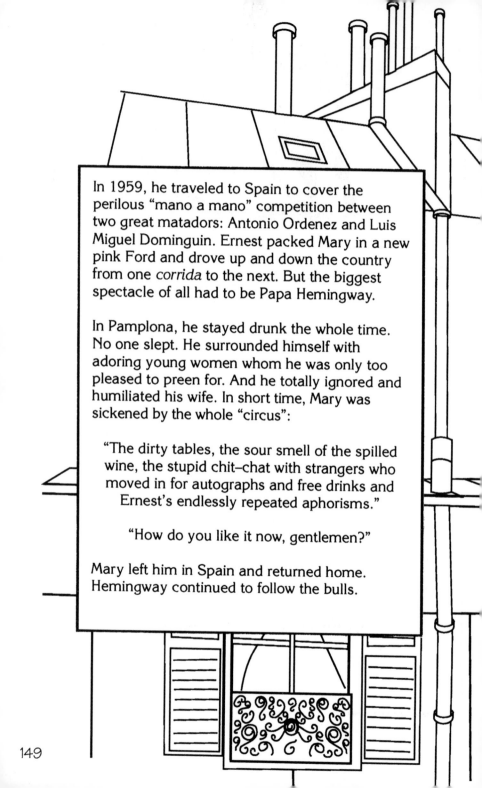

In 1959, he traveled to Spain to cover the perilous "mano a mano" competition between two great matadors: Antonio Ordenez and Luis Miguel Dominguin. Ernest packed Mary in a new pink Ford and drove up and down the country from one *corrida* to the next. But the biggest spectacle of all had to be Papa Hemingway.

In Pamplona, he stayed drunk the whole time. No one slept. He surrounded himself with adoring young women whom he was only too pleased to preen for. And he totally ignored and humiliated his wife. In short time, Mary was sickened by the whole "circus":

"The dirty tables, the sour smell of the spilled wine, the stupid chit–chat with strangers who moved in for autographs and free drinks and Ernest's endlessly repeated aphorisms."

"How do you like it now, gentlemen?"

Mary left him in Spain and returned home. Hemingway continued to follow the bulls.

That winter he was back in Havana trying to write about the summer. The article was supposed to run thirty thousand words. It was now three times that length. And Hemingway refused to edit. Or he was no longer able.

"I can see the words on the page for only ten or twelve minutes, before my eyes cut out...".

Aaron Hotchner agreed to come down to Cuba in June to help. He was shocked by the changes in Papa. Ernest was thinner, almost "whittled" away. The front of his head was bald, and his beard hadn't been trimmed in months. He wasn't drinking. He ate little. But he worried a great deal.

Hemingway worried about Fidel Castro's revolution. The new Cuban government vilified Americans. Worst of all, Hemingway was unsure of his writing. And he argued against every one of Hotchner's cuts—in terms that often made no sense. Things were even worse deep inside, where they didn't show:

"It's like living in a Kafka nightmare.
I act cheerful as always but am not.
I'm bone tired and very beat-up emotionally."

The depression and paranoia continued. In November 1960, Ernest was admitted for treatment at the Mayo Clinic in Rochester, Minnesota. He registered under his doctor's name. Over a period of several weeks, he received electric-shock treatments—between 11 and 15 doses. But he received little or no counseling.

Shock wipes out memory for some weeks or months. Hemingway was not warned. And he panicked. Memory, he said, was his literary "capital." How would he ever work again? When he was released, he returned to his home in Ketchum, Idaho. Gregory described the house in these words:

"Set well back from the road, it was an almost bunker-like blockhouse, built of poured concrete to last two hundred years, an ideal buttress against the world, and as safe a refuge as could be found for a paranoid."

Hemingway desperately tried to write. But the muses were deaf to his pleas. And religion was no help. He believed in God, but he couldn't pray for himself anymore. He said he had become too hardened.

"What does a man care about? Staying healthy. Working good. Eating and drinking with his friends. Enjoying himself in bed. I haven't any of them."

It was better to go out in a blaze of light than having your body worn out and old and all your illusions shattered.

In April 1961, Mary found her husband cradling his shotgun in his arms. She persuaded him to fly out to the Mayo Clinic for more treatment. On the way he tried to walk into the moving propeller of a small plane.

Hemingway received another full course of electric-shock therapy. In private, he accused Mary of trying to have him sent away to jail or killed. But to the doctors he pretended to be completely cured.

Now he knew what he must do. For Ernest Hemingway there could be not turning back.

"If I can't exist on my own terms, then existence is impossible."

On his next to last day on earth Hemingway and Mary went out for dinner at a local restaurant in Ketchum. Ernest was convinced a pair of traveling salesmen at a nearby table were FBI agents on his tail. He made Mary leave immediately.

That night, she began to sing an Italian folk song to herself while undressing for bed. Papa joined in for a while. Then, before turning off the lights, he whispered, "Good night, my kitten." And he went to bed. Those were the last words Hemingway ever said to anyone.

Early in the morning of July 2, 1961, Ernest Miller Hemingway woke up and went downstairs. In the foyer of the main entrance to the house, he aimed a shotgun at his head and fired.

Hemingway's suicide produced more questions than answers. Suddenly the world was forced to see the man's whole life in a different light.Critic Edmund Wilson was deeply shocked:

"It is as if a whole corner of my generation had
suddenly and horribly collapsed."

The great matador Juan Belmonte not only approved—aging, in retirement, he soon followed Don Ernesto's example:

"Well done..."

Those who knew Hemingway best recalled him in different ways. His son Gregory wrote:

"The man I remembered was kind, gentle,
elemental in his vastness, tormented beyond endurance."

Jack Hemingway, his eldest son:

"I keep thinking what a wonderful old man he would have been if
he learned how. I don't think he faced up to being old."

Martha Gellhorn, his rebellious third wife:

"He was a genius, that uneasy word, not so much in what he wrote
as in how he wrote. He liberated our written language."

Brother Leicester:

"He wanted to be more than Superman.
He wanted to be Superman's older brother."

Mary Welsh Hemingway was married to him longer than any woman. Despite the suffering she went through living with him, this is what she remembered:

"His enjoyment of everything and his zest for life, and his
exuberance. Lots of people maintain that he was a great, bravado
boy, boastful, and a big, boisterous public figure...What people saw
as bravado could well have been disguise,
an attempt to escape from shyness."

154

Whoever he really was, Ernest Hemingway was able to touch the world the way few people ever do in their lifetime. He was buried in Ketchum on July 5, 1961. His grave had a fine view of the mountains. Most of the enemies he had made, and most of his friends, were dead. Now he would join them, at rest at last, in the earth that he loved.

All his life he sailed a course that led to the "undiscovered country" of death. Under different circumstances perhaps Hemingway could've accepted his sensitivity in all its richness and contradiction. Perhaps he would not have made such stringent demands on himself and the people around him. And perhaps he might've found some island in the stream of life where he finally felt at peace.

Hemingway once said that he felt no regrets for what he had done. Only for what he had not done. Maybe he wanted to believe this. What is certain is that he died the way he wanted to live. On his own terms.

Perhaps the scope of his art was narrow in some ways. But like the Gulf Stream that he knew so well, it went deep. Sometimes deeper than even he could fathom.

There is a final irony. The priest at the funeral was asked to read several passages from the Book of Ecclesiastes. Hemingway always believed these words from the Bible served to put men in their proper place.

But the priest only read the lines that said, "Vanity of vanities, quoted the Preacher...all is vanity."

He left out the passage that talked about how one generation passes away, and another generation comes, but the earth abides for ever. And that the sun also rises...

"I am glad we do not have to kill the stars. Imagine if each day a man must try to kill the moon. The moon runs away. But imagine if a man each day should have to try and kill the sun. We are born lucky. Yes, we are born lucky."

# FOR FURTHER READING

All of Hemingway's published prose and fiction writings
are available from the publishing company of **Charles Scribner's Sons**,
New York. These include:

- BY-LINE: ERNEST HEMINGWAY
- THE COMPLETE SHORT STORIES OF ERNEST HEMINGWAY
- DEATH IN THE AFTERNOON
- A FAREWELL TO ARMS
- FOR WHOM THE BELL TOLLS
- THE GARDEN OF EDEN
- A MOVEABLE FEAST
- THE OLD MAN AND THE SEA
- THE SUN ALSO RISES

To learn more about Hemingway, his life, times and works, read the following:

Baker, Carlos. **ERNEST HEMINGWAY: A LIFE STORY**. New
York: Charles Scribner's Sons, 1969

Brian, Denis. **THE TRUE GEN**. New York: Grove Press, 1986

Fenton, Charles A. **THE APPRENTICESHIP OF ERNEST
HEMINGWAY: THE EARLY YEARS**. New York: Viking Press,
1954

Hotchner, A.E. **PAPA HEMINGWAY**. New York: Random
House, 1966

Kert, Bernice. **THE HEMINGWAY WOMEN**. New York: W.W.
Norton, 1983

Lynn, Kenneth S. **HEMINGWAY**. New York: Simon &
Schuster, 1987

Meyers, Jeffrey. **HEMINGWAY: A BIOGRAPHY**. New York:
Harper & Row, 1985

# INDEX